BRITAIN'S
HISTORIC COAST

BRITAIN'S HISTORIC COAST

Alison Gale

TEMPUS

First published 2000

PUBLISHED IN THE UNITED KINGDOM BY:

Tempus Publishing Ltd
The Mill, Brimscombe Port
Stroud, Gloucestershire GL5 2QG

PUBLISHED IN THE UNITED STATES OF AMERICA BY:

Tempus Publishing Inc.
2A Cumberland Street
Charleston, SC 29401

Tempus books are available in France, Germany and Belgium
from the following addresses:

Tempus Publishing Group	Tempus Publishing Group	Tempus Publishing Group
21 Avenue de la République	Gustav-Adolf-Straße 3	Place de L'Alma 4/5
37300 Joué-lès-Tours	99084 Erfurt	1200 Brussels
FRANCE	GERMANY	BELGIUM

British Library Cataloguing in Publication Data.
A catalogue record for this book is available from the British Library.

ISBN 0 7524 1456 9

Typesetting and origination by Tempus Publishing.
PRINTED AND BOUND IN GREAT BRITAIN.

Contents

Preface

Reading the opening passages of Herman Melville's *Moby Dick* was for me like looking into a mirror.

> But look! here come more crowds, pacing straight for the water, and seemingly bound for a dive. Strange! Nothing will content them but the extremist limit of the land; loitering under the shady lee of yonder warehouse will not suffice. No. They must get just as nigh the water as they possibly can without falling in.

This book has been written for all those who cannot keep from the coast and who have the curiosity to wonder at fine townscapes, industrial ports, derelict harbours and ruinous sites from prehistoric earthworks to the concrete coast defences of World War Two.

Its structure owes much to a project which I undertook for the North of England Museums Service. In examining the maritime collections held by museums from Berwick-upon-Tweed to Staithes I had first to ask what was *maritime history*. The scope to think countrywide came with completing chapters on archaeology for 16 volumes of the Joint Nature Conservation Committees *Coastal Directories Series*.

During those projects Valerie Fenwick and I considered the need for archaeological guides to the coast. There seemed two needs: to give sound background to those with responsibility for managing the coast and to raise public awareness and enjoyment. The first need should have been met by the survey *England's Coastal Heritage*, produced by English Heritage and the Royal Commission on the Historical Monuments of England, and we were faced with the more pressing need to draw attention to the shortcomings in the protection and interpretation of our shipwreck heritage. We responded by writing *Historic Shipwrecks* which was published by Tempus in 1998. A second joint effort proved impracticable. However, my thoughts in this present work have without doubt been informed by my long hours with Valerie amid sunny dunes, on windy cliffs, in icy estuaries and closeted in the warmth of tea shops and curry houses.

This book dips with delight into many subjects. To explore them I have drawn heavily on those stretches of coast on which I have worked and lived. There is no pretence at encyclopaedic coverage but a hope that the text and illustrations open the readers' eyes to see the wealth of the past which is visible on any part of the British coast. It is written for visitors to that coast and anyone who is interested in the ways that man has used the fringe of sea and land from the stone age to the computer age.

October 1999

Illustrations

Text figures

Colour plates

Acknowledgements

Many thanks to Jilly for teasing meaning from my sentences and laughter from me.

For permission to reproduce illustrations:
Clifford Bloomfield
A Croome, Edna Lumb Artistic Trust
Garry Momber, Hampshire & Wight Trust for Maritime Archaeology
Gustav Milne
Premier Marinas Ltd
Southern Water

The following are thanked for supplying information on the diverse topics within this book:
R Alcock, Brewer's Walk, Weymouth. S Beckett, Poole Museum Service. R. Benvie, Montrose Museum & Art Gallery. A Credlund, Town Docks Museum, Hull. T. Ellis, Coastguard Museum, Bridlington. Forth Ports PLC. M Hunter, Osborne House. F Guest, Arbroath Museum. Capt. R Leask. Dr Colin Martin, University of St Andrews. E Meechan, HM Customs & Excise Museum, Greenock. Milford Haven Museum. Moray Council Museums Service. National Fishing Heritage Centre, Grimsby. C. Osborne, Maldon Crystal Salt. R. Pickles, Whitby Museum. Porthmadog Maritime Museum. Premier Marinas Ltd., Owain Roberts, M. Stammers, Merseyside Maritime Musuem. D. Strachan, Essex County Council. C Spendlove, Portsmouth Museums & Records Service. Swallow Fish Ltd. Tourist Information Centres: Aberystwyth, Bournemouth, Deal, Folkestone, Hastings, Helston, Hertford, Milford Haven, Newcastle-upon-Tyne, Plymouth, Swanage, Wareham, Weymouth, Whitby. Wildlife & Wetland Trust, Slimbridge. B Wilson, Tankerness Museum.

1 *When Edwin Gifford steered from Woodbridge Quay on the River Deben, passing boats called out to the 'Viking Boat,' and up went the united cry of her wool and leather clad crew 'Not Viking, Saxon'. They were sailing and rowing* Sae Wilfing, *a modern scale recreation of a 89ft (27m) ship excavated from a seventh-century burial mound near by*

1 Life by the sea

For though you should know every entry and every sounding, the first hour in every flood when your craft can safely go over the banks...yet you do not possess that piece of water unless you see moving upon it the fullness of its past. Belloc, 1925. *The Cruise of the* Nona

For any island the coast will come centre stage in the momentous events whose retelling in fact and fiction become the nation's history. So the wooden hulls crunching onto the beaches of Sussex carried William ashore with his mighty Norman knights; Drake bowled on Plymouth Hoe as the Spanish Armada approached; great shoreline defences were raised against French invasions which never came; and the Little Ships gathered in Ramsgate to make their incredible rescue from Dunkirk. The 'visible legacies' on the coast tell not so much of these single dates in history but a long story of people making use of the coast.

From the time of the earliest hunters the coast has provided a very special place to live. It offers a good climate with food from many environments, including fish from the sea, shellfish from beaches, birds and eggs from cliff-faces, plants from marshes, and crops from the land. Promontories can be made defensible positions, while rocks and minerals are easily found in cliff-face exposures. The sea is readily available for transporting people and goods and with them travel ideas, knowledge and fashions. The technology of boat and shipbuilding enabled coastal communities to reach out and win resources from across the sea and, in recent decades, from the seabed itself.

In every age, with ingenuity and hard labour, coastal dwellers created structures and devices to help them get the best out of their environment. Stretching the limits of their technological ability, they used the coast and sea to supply resources, to dispose of waste, for transport, for leisure and to defend themselves. This book explores the present coast by explaining these past activities and the remains that they have left behind. Discovering, investigating and explaining such physical remains is the task of archaeologists, from those who specialise in prehistory to those who focus on the industrial age. Chapter two explains the challenge of studying sites which may be on land, in the intertidal zone or beneath the sea. It also sets out the different uses of the sea as a route to understanding the coastal archaeology. The rest of this chapter gives a brief overview of what has been discovered about life on the coast since the last Ice Age.

The conundrum of archaeology

There is no right answer for archaeologists as they seek to build a picture of how people lived, worked, played, worshipped and died. Innovative scientific techniques, new data and fresh ideas mean that their interpretation of the, sometimes sparse, surviving remains need frequent revision.

Like everything else, archaeology has its own history and amongst all the modernity some old things are still prominent. Before modern analysis began providing absolute dates for artefacts and sites, archaeologists used relative dating based on the idea of progress in technology. Thus the Stone Age, divided into Palaeolithic (old stone), Mesolithic and Neolithic, was followed by the Bronze Age and then the Iron Age. These terms are still commonly used despite their obvious shortcoming as an explanation of changing cultures. In reality new materials and designs supplement rather than supplant existing ones. For example, the ability to make bronze tools did not stop people hunting with flint-tipped arrows, just as in today's kitchen plastic spoons and chopping boards have not eliminated wooden utensils. In addition, change comes at different times in different places. The Mesolithic in southern England gives way to the Neolithic in the fifth millennium BC but in Scotland it continues to the third millenium BC. The Roman invasion in 43 BC brings Britain into the historic period, the time of written records. However, the culture of Rome had so little impact on the north of Scotland that the Iron Age there is not broken until the coasts were raided and settled by Vikings in the eighth century.

Palaeolithic

The story of today's island Britain and her peoples begins around 12,000 years ago as the last Ice Age was coming to an end. Like earlier ice ages the Devensian Glacial had seen snow and ice build up over large areas of the earth. The water which they contained could not flow back to the oceans and so the level of the sea dropped. The region that is now Britain was connected to Europe, not by a narrow land bridge but by great plains in the area of the present North Sea.

While it is clear that modern man, *Homo sapiens*, was living in Britain, little is now left of his Palaeolithic landscape. Much of it was scoured away by the ice sheets which advanced far southwards around 26,000 BC. The rivers, beside which people are likely to have lived, have also long since changed their courses. The remains of camp sites, found in Britain today, suggest that hunting groups were ranging this far across the plains. Some scant remains have also been found in caves, a few of which are near today's coast. Kent's Cavern in Torquay, Devon, contained flint tools and animal bones which were dated by radiocarbon to the 27th millennium BC. A date of about 25,000 BC has been suggested for a young man who was ritually buried with ivory rods, bracelets and perforated shells in Goat's Cave, Glamorgan. The red ochre sprinkled over the remains led his Hanoverian (1823) discoverers to dub their find, with some error of sexing, the Red Lady of Paviland.

Would the people who used Kent's Cavern and Goat Cave have been coastal dwellers? The difficulty lies in correlating debatable dates for human activity with models for sea level and the position of the contemporary coast. There is no doubt, however, that their predecessors knew and used the resources of the coast. The oldest human remains in Britain date to about 500,000 BC. They come from Boxgrove, Sussex, where excavators found that tools had been made from beach flints.

Around 15,000 BC the last Ice Age began to end; the ice sheets alternately retreated and advanced during a period of fluctuating climate which lasted for about 5000 years. Plants and then animals accustomed to tundra-like conditions, such as elk, reindeer, red deer and horse, recolonised the area of Britain. Unfortunately knowledge of the people who, with a better climate, could once again move northwards, is predominantly based on finds preserved inside caves. Little is known of their use of open land for homes.

Mesolithic

After about 10,000 BC the large plains would have been rich with grasses, roamed by herds of grazing animals and peopled by hunters. The warming conditions also unlocked the water held in ice-sheets and snowfields. As it flowed from the land so the sea level began to rise, flooding the low-lying plains. Around 11,000 BC outlying land such as Orkney was isolated by the rising water and about 8000 years ago island Britain was separated from mainland Europe. In contrast to the modern landscape water dominated the post-glacial landscape. The Lake District and Scottish lochs are lasting reminders of the glaciation, but open water and marshes would also have abounded in lowland areas with rivers freely flowing and overflowing where there is now carefully drained farmland and little marsh.

Water, inland and coastal, was a focus for people's activities and settlements. Food was easily to hand: shellfish and fish of course, but also animals and birds which came to drink and feed. Equipped with weapons and tools of wood, flint and antler, families were able to feed and clothe themselves by hunting and gathering. This Mesolithic way of life, which had no need for permanent settlements, was the only means of survival until the ability to cultivate crops was learnt. Even after farming had been adopted, towards the end of the fifth millennium BC, the hunter-gatherer lifestyle persisted, perhaps as an alternative but quite probably as a supplement.

The most common Mesolithic remains in Britain consist of stone and antler tools, and rubbish such as butchered animal bones and marine shells. Hearths are recognisable remains of campsites while evidence for shelters comprise little more than post holes which are suggestive of only lightweight structures, possibly portable homes such as tents. Ideas for the way in which groups lived range through use and abandonment of camps possibly following grazing animals, the establishment of base settlements with specialised camps for hunting and butchering, and the seasonal use of camps.

Archaeology is always about attempting to reconstruct the whole from a small surviving part. For the Mesolithic the problem is twofold. In common with other periods only a small number of the places originally used for living and hunting have been found, but much of the Mesolithic landscape has also disappeared under the sea. Around 6000 BC rising sea level created island Britain, separate from mainland Europe. The vast plains lost to the North Sea and the coastal lands now beneath the Bristol Channel and the

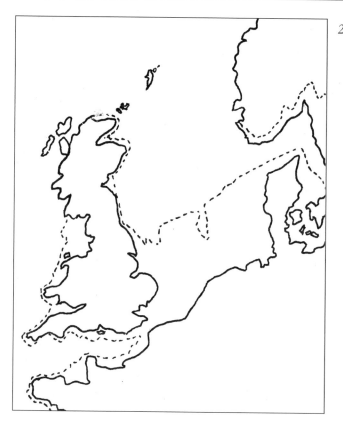

2 *The conjectured coastline around 9,000 years ago. Britain was a peninsula on the north European coast, joined by great plains to the areas which are now the Low Countries and Denmark*

estuaries of the south coast can be imagined when it is known that between 7000 and 5000 BC sea level was perhaps 52-36m (170-120ft) lower than today (**2**).

Artefacts such as a wooden paddle from Starr Carr, Yorkshire and an antler harpoon from Whitburn, County Durham, show how boats and tools were being made to exploit watery environments whether coastal or inland. However locating and investigating the ephemeral settlement remains of early Mesolithic coastal dwellers will require the foremost techniques of underwater survey and archaeological excavation.

Some parts of today's coast have revealed clues to Mesolithic coastal activity. Discarded shells make up the bulk of rubbish tips, called middens. The quantities are staggering. Some 7250 kg (16,000lb) excavated from Culverwell, Portland Dorset, is reckoned as the remains of sufficient shellfish to feed a family of eight for 150 days. So much for believing that Mesolithic families or groups had no ties to semi-permanent or permanent homes. The Inner Hebridean island of Oronsay has six middens at one site. Middens at Morton, near the mouth of the Tay, Fife, show that in addition to red and roe deer, auroch and pig, the community enjoyed the coastal resources: collecting whelks and mussels; catching seabirds; and fishing, probably from a boat in deep water, for cod and sturgeon.

Neolithic

What brought change to the Mesolithic lifestyle is uncertain. What characterises the Neolithic is the first appearance of cultivated wheat, new tools, such as polished stone axes, and the building of large structures requiring community effort.

The ability to grow crops emerged first in the Near East. By exchange of ideas or movement of people the practice reached Britain by sometime in the fifth millennium BC. It was not off-the-peg farming, which today implies specialist producers, permanently managing large areas of land, and feeding consumers at a distance. Their stone axes were essential tools for clearing woodland so that seeds could be sown, but once the land was exhausted or became unmanageable it was abandoned. Enclosures comprising concentric banks and ditches, with wooden palisades, were built on high and low ground, some encircling large acreages. Their uses appear to have included coralling cattle, enclosing settlements and providing market places, but also defending people, property or territory.

Until recently knowledge of Neolithic peoples derived from study of their most robust structures. These chambers of stone and earth played a part in ritual and were used as communal tombs (**3**). Across Britain there are thousands of surviving examples. By identifying groups of similar designs and the number of burials within them archaeologists have put forward ideas for the division of territory and size of communities. Tombs on the coast have even brought hypotheses over the control of the coast and use of these communal buildings as seamarks. Far more certain proof of Neolithic seafaring comes from the wide spread of polished axes. These show sea voyages were made to the Continent and between islands within the archipelago which is now the British Isles.

In the last 30 years the Somerset Levels have provided new and remarkable insight into the way that early farmers could use coastal wetlands. In the centuries before 4500 BC the sea filled the Bristol Channel and flowed into the low land of the Somerset Levels. From around 4500 sand dunes developed which prevented the tidal flooding of this marshland. Neolithic communities began using the Levels as they turned from brackish to fresh water swamp. Higher ground, forming dry islands, was used for settlements and crops. To help people or animals cross the swamp-like ground, communities built wooden and hurdle trackways, kilometres long. The many unique finds made here include a long bow. Such a bow, with a 100m range, might have added water birds and mammals from the marsh fringe to the diet.

The most easily understood image of Neolithic settlements comes from Orkney. Here the local building material was stone and the most famous group of houses was found at Skara Brae (**4**). Coastal erosion uncovered the homes which looked nearly as complete as when they had been first engulfed by sand dunes. Also on Orkney similar houses have been found at Knap of Howar (Papa Westray), Rinjo (Rousay), and Links of Noltland (Westray), while comparable oval houses have been found on Shetland at Scourd of Brouster and Ness of Gruting. In addition to growing wheat and raising cattle the house-dwellers were using the natural resources of the coast: shellfish, fish and birds. The sea may even have made up for materials that were not available on land, as the houses may have been roofed using either driftwood or bones from stranded whales.

3   One of the Grey Cairns of Camster which lie five miles inland from Lybster, Highland. The waist-high entrance (far left) leads to a stone built chamber. Early farmers worked together to construct such ritual and funerary monuments

Changes are apparent from about 3500 BC when some regions began to revert to woodland as communities became focused on the most fertile areas. The large monuments became disused, with some tombs actually being blocked up. A new form of monumental building, the stone circle, began at the end of that millennium (**5**). With the exception of one example in Brittany, these are confined to the British Isles, the Stones of Stenness on Orkney being among the earliest.

Bronze Age

The ability to extract metal from ore and cast objects was learnt in the Near East before 4500 BC. The resulting 'copper age' cannot be traced in Britain. Its absence is not the result of contact with the mainland ceasing, since European copper tools were well-enough known to be copied in the traditional material of flint. The first home-manufactures in metal are of bronze, the alloy of approximately eight parts copper to one part tin. The most commonly found are axes, daggers and awls, many of which may have had symbolic rather than functional use.

A coastal Bronze Age copper mine has been excavated on the Great Orme in Gwynedd. There are 70m of tunnels and shafts in which fire was used to fracture the rock, and then antler picks to release the ore. Beach cobbles, presumably from the shores of the promontory, were used to crush the ore (**6**). Since scrap bronze was certainly carried by boat it is possible to imagine copper ingots or finished products shipped coastwise from

4   Neolithic House, Orkney. The village at Skara Brae was revealed by coastal erosion. Its now roofless dry-stone houses are fitted with stone furnishings such as box beds and this dresser

North Wales. The repertoire of bronze toolmakers expanded until it included long daggers, called rapiers, which may have been the precursors to more familiar swords.

A preference for bronze may have gone hand-in-hand with a passion for wine and pot-smoking. A new form of pottery appears at about the same time as metalworking. Based on analysis of plant remains, the most recent explanation of these 'beakers' is as containers for a mead like drink, and of their decoration as the mark of hemp cords, or cannabis.

The beakers, usually containing human remains, are frequently found in graves. The earliest are cut into the fills of disused Neolithic enclosures and tombs as communal tombs gave way to individual burials and cremations. Later graves were marked by round cairns or barrows often placed in groups, many of which are close to larger monuments of standing stones. These cemeteries also include graves with no structure above ground level. With some 30,000 known barrows, the archaeological landscape of the Bronze Age is dominated by death. The prominent positioning of barrow groups suggests that the land was divided into territories, perhaps based on cattle ranching. Traces of early settlements have only been preserved where later barrows have protected the ground from destructive activities such as ploughing. Similar preservation has been found beneath coastal sand dunes.

The Bronze Age landscape has been mapped by fieldwalking and aerial photographs. Dartmoor was among the first areas to show low field boundaries of stone which divided large tracts of land. The enclosed areas were subdivided and linked to round houses. In the later Bronze Age, settlements and burials appear more closely based on family groups or small communities with the round house as the principle dwelling. Smaller versions formed stores or workshops. Round houses were formed of a circular wattle and daub

5   *The surviving stones in the Ring of Brogar, Orkney, now dominate a neck of land between the Lochs of Harray and Stenness*

6   *Metal-working display at the Great Orme, Bronze Age copper mine. Top right is a beach cobble for grinding ore and top left a crucible. In the foreground are axe heads in their moulds, hafted axes and a copper ingot*

wall and a conical reed-thatched roof carried by posts and rafters. They were spacious with an apex some 8m high and floors exceeding 100 sq m (1076 sqft).

Iron Age

The technology of iron-making was known in Britain from about 700 BC. The following centuries are characterised not only by this additional metal but by changes in the settlement of the landscape. While archaeological investigation has found the new artefacts and sites, without written records to tell their story the cause of change remains the subject of imagination, and theory.

From around 500 BC the design of iron objects shows close contact with Europe, especially between the area of the Humber and Holland. People may have migrated, or perhaps tribal leaders travelled overseas and after returning home emulated other cultures with new rituals, such as burial with chariots. Continental imports supply the evidence for ports, for example at Redcliff on the Humber. Hengistbury Head, Dorset, is recognised as a trading port from ceramic imports, which demonstrate close contacts with Gaul in the first century BC. Iron Age coins from Kent, themselves evidence of the region's prominence in trade, actually depict a native vessel. However, although Bronze Age plank boats have been found in Britain, no comparable Iron Age vessels (pre-dating the Roman period) have yet been discovered.

In this period peat growth on higher land, caused by a wetter and cooler climate, covered many areas previously used by Bronze Age communities. The rising sea level was also reducing the coastal plain; stone field boundaries are among the features of the drowned Bronze Age landscape that can be traced in the shallow waters surrounding the Isles of Scilly. The tension caused by an increased density of population on the fewer fertile areas has been suggested as a reason for the construction of defended settlements. These range from earth and ditch ramparts enclosing many hectares of hilltop to sites of less than an acre secured, for instance, by a bank across the neck of a promontory. Coastal examples, especially numerous on the rugged cliffs of Cornwall and South West Wales, can be found in many parts of the country and their absence from areas such as the Yorkshire may be no more than the result of extensive cliff erosion. In most areas timber and thatch round houses provided the domestic buildings (**7**). Dry-stone structures, however, characterise the Atlantic coast of Scotland. There is a variety of forts and towers, called brochs (**30**). The visual dominance of brochs may have led early studies to undervalue ancillary buildings while, at Underhoull on Shetland, it was the excavation of a later settlement which revealed a small stone house contemporary with the brochs.

A specific coastal industry can be traced in the remains of salt making sites. In Lincolnshire, evidence from Ingoldmells has been dated as early as the fourth century BC, while twentieth-century storms at Mablethorpe have exposed associated rush-floored huts. In Essex salt making sites, known as redhills, are numbered in hundreds.

7   *Iron Age house reconstructed at the Somerset Peat Centre following excavation in the surrounding Levels*

The Roman province

In AD 43 the Roman invasion force made the short sea crossing to establish a bridgehead at Richborough in Kent, the region which traded most closely across the Channel. The Imperial Legions advanced rapidly through the territories of successive tribes along the south coast, targeting any resistance based on the prominent hillforts. Military occupation was gradually consolidated by the construction of forts linked by roads. Changes in the coastline have distorted the original system. The Peddars Way now ends abruptly at Holme-next-the-Sea but may once have linked Norfolk and Lincolnshire. Signal stations are crumbling from the Yorkshire cliffs while forts on the line of Hadrian's Wall now lie in the Solway Firth.

Sea transport supported campaigns into more remote regions. The 2nd Legion, for example, was stationed in Devon at Exeter, for which downriver Topsham was a port, and after AD 74 in Wales at Caerleon, Gwent, where remains of port facilities have also been found. Supply forts on the River Tyne (**26**) and Forth supported campaigns into the eastern coastal plain of Scotland, where the most northerly remains of a marching camp lie at Keith.

Excavation in London has revealed quays and warehouses capable of handling large quantities of cargo (**46**). Merchant shipping is likely to have prospered in other military-controlled ports. In West Sussex a harbour and granaries at Fishbourne on Chichester Harbour are believed to have passed into civilian use, and trade may have created the wealth represented by the fine palace nearby. Cargoes probably included coastal products, since salt and pottery and tile making sites have been found around the Harbour. Evidence of similar industries survives around Poole Harbour while urban rubbish tips show that oysters were harvested; Lincolnshire has many salt-making sites and Upchurch, now marshland on the north Kent coast, has given its name to locally-made pottery. On the Severn Estuary the erosion of mud flats, on the seaward side of present sea defences, has revealed Roman drainage systems by which land had been claimed for agriculture.

Beyond Roman occupation

Roman control was never permanently established beyond the Tyne-Solway gap. Far to the north, Shetland, Orkney, Highland and the Outer Hebrides were untouched by the military campaigns; Roman-style artefacts are curiosities suggesting very occasional, and perhaps indirect, contact with regions to the south. While the Romans referred to all tribes beyond the frontier as Picts, today the name is applied to those of Shetland, Orkney and the north east of mainland Scotland. Ideas of Pictish maritime prowess are supported by the existence of coastal centres, some of which occupy older Iron Age forts such as Burghead and Cullykhan on the Moray Firth. However, while Pictish areas are rich in stones decoratively inscribed with symbols, their domestic buildings are harder to trace. Evidence comes from remote coastal landscapes. At Buckquoy in Orkney remains of a Pictish settlement have been found beneath a Viking Age farmstead of the ninth century. Here as on other sites there seems to have been a transition from Pictish to Norse artefacts following the first arrival of Scandinavians in the eighth century; this blending of cultures is also evident in the mixture of building techniques observed in the boats which have been excavated from graves. On Shetland such a cultural transition is not evident as excavations of Viking Age settlements at Underhoull and Jarlshoff have revealed only uncertain examples of Pictish houses beneath.

The Viking raids may have contributed to mainland Pictish areas succumbing to the control by Scots, whose power-base lay to the south east. The Northern Isles, however, remained under the Scandinavians until formally passed to Scotland in 1468. Hoards of precious metals show that wealth was accumulated in Orkney, where excavations have revealed parts of Viking Age Kirkwall, a trading port on sea routes between Scandinavia, Ireland and the Mediterranean.

Any effect of the Roman withdrawal in AD 410 shows little trace in the archaeological record of remote regions like Cornwall. Overseas contacts must have continued since pottery imported from the Mediterranean and Africa has been found on the prominent coastal site of Tintagel, which has parallels in both Wales and Scotland. In contrast the South East suffered economically with towns and manufacturing seeming to decline; the Roman army had after all been a consumer of many goods. A fifth-century cemetery at Mucking on the Thames shows that Germanic peoples had begun settling the region, while in the sixth century the reviving fortunes of the Kent area are also shown by grave goods, from Dover and Faversham, which include exotic objects imported from the Mediterranean.

Christianity, like earlier but undocumented beliefs, was carried to the coast of Britain by sea. In 597 the Pope sent 40 missionaries while others came independently, and at earlier dates, from Ireland, especially to Scotland and the Northern Isles. Small islets and cliff-top sites were chosen by many religious communities and by holy men living as hermits. Their remoteness has ensured the survival of banks and stone walls that enclosed the settlements, and on Orkney the place-name 'papa' is linked to such sites. Coastal monasteries such as Whithorn, Dumfries & Galloway, became destinations for pilgrims and focal points for both travellers and imported goods.

A clinker-built Saxon ship has been excavated at Sutton Hoo, Suffolk. The grave goods inside, including weapons and domestic objects made by highly-skilled craftsmen, show the status and wealth enjoyed by the ruler of a coastal kingdom. Modern experiments have demonstrated the rowing and sailing capability of this ship (**1**), and shown the probable function of a tenth century Saxon boat found at Graveney, Kent. Measuring 44ft by 13ft (13.6m x 4m) this boat was well-suited to carrying river and coastal cargoes. Growing ports have been revealed by excavations in London, Ipswich and Southampton which have recovered foerign glassware and pottery. From the end of the eighth century the flourishing religious centres and prospering coastal towns became the targets of Viking raids. Southern England was nevertheless an Anglo-Saxon kingdom when the Norman Duke William launched his invasion ships in 1066.

From Domesday

Twenty years after defeating King Harold, William I ordered a survey of his kingdom. The resulting Domesday Book is largely an inventory of agriculture wealth in which salt-making sites are included among the assets of coastal land. In the following centuries, as the number of surviving documents grows, there is increasing information about such coastal activities. Ports were more and more involved in foreign trade; in time, larger trading centres drew to them produce shipped from smaller ports and stimulated exploitation of diverse coastal resources to supply both their manufactories and foreign markets, and not least their own populations.

Coastal towns rose and fell with the market for shipped goods, the fortunes of the foreign ports to which they traded, and the success of their natural harbours in withstanding tempests and the invidious attack of siltation or erosion. Like Sandwich on the Kentish Stour and Goseford on Suffolk's Deben innumerable medieval ports are now little heard of backwaters. While such ports decayed London expanded, benefitting from the commodious Thames and closeness to the great market cities of the Low Countries. By the fourteenth century the capital dominated the export of wool and cloth, England's principal trade.

During the sixteenth century East Coast ports re-established themselves in foreign trade with the Baltic, a source of raw materials and market for manufactures. London became involved, once more, in direct trade to the Mediterranean while ports in the South West developed the Newfoundland fisheries. In Scotland, now quiet coastal towns were then enjoying their status as burghs, and engaging in profitable trade with the continent which enabled construction of harbours such as at Portsoy (**colour plate 10**). The seventeenth century brought opportunities for the western ports as the Spanish monopoly in the Americas was broken: British plantations started in the West Indies, settlements began in Virginia and emigrants populated New England. Cromwell's 1651 Navigation Act claimed shipping as England's right by requiring that foreign imports be carried only in English ships with largely English crews. During wars with the Dutch, the capture of literally thousands of the most well-designed cargo ships available, fluits, finally provided English merchants with the right tools for this trade. In the coming century British shipyards would replace these with new tonnage well-suited to cargo-carrying.

The eighteenth and nineteenth centuries have left a highly visible imprint on the coast. Landowners and merchants invested in entrepreneurial ventures to exploit its resources. Their capital, combined with innovative engineering skills and new materials, created installations which were both greater in scale and longer-lived than earlier industrial sites. They extended the seaward boundary of coastal activities: building harbour piers into the sea and lighthouses on distant rocks. While lighthouses and other navigation marks helped protect the small investments of thousands of people in ships and cargoes, the creation of life-saving organisations was the work of pure philanthropy. Government recognised the importance of the coast and ensured regulation, adding, for example, Coast Guards to the existing Customs & Excise service. Similarly, the government was able to establish a coherent system of fortifications to defend against invasion. At the same time the coast became a destination for holidays and day-trips, so enshrining itself in the national consciousness as a place for escape and frivolity.

From this wild coastal cacophony the later chapters of this book distil out individual activities for explanation. Before this, Chapter two looks at the present coast and the type of archaeological remains which it has preserved.

2   The coast in time and space

...take out the plug and let the water drain away, leaving long ago valleys, hills, riverbeds and forests exposed again to the seagull's eye. Harrison, 1986. *The Channel.*

In Britain no-one lives more than some 70 miles from the sea, and for some areas it is more significant than for others. In Scotland, for example, where sea lochs cut deep into the land, the coast is estimated as 5140 miles (8270 km) long compared with only 2770 miles (4452 km) for the combined coast of England and Wales. Yet in recent years a growing number of archaeologists have become concerned that their studies have neglected the coast. In the late 1980s the database maps of archaeological discoveries, maintained by local authorities and called Sites & Monuments Records, were often blank for many miles of coast. This did not necessarily mean that no remains survived from the past but only that no-one had made the effort to record them.

Local Sites & Monuments Records began back in the 1970s by collating a hotch-potch of information including writings of antiquarians from the eighteenth century, museum records of artefacts, sites mapped since the nineteenth century by the Ordnance Survey, and the work of local archaeological societies published in their periodicals. Since then a great deal of work has focused on recording sites threatened by building development, and as a result rural areas including the open coast remained unexplored. Increasingly, however, systematic surveys have aimed to redress the imbalance by targeting areas such as wetlands and uplands. These surveys use techniques like aerial photography to study the whole landscape, rather than specific sites or periods.

In the 1990s a number of factors combined to push the coast up the archaeological agenda. Firstly, unrivalled discoveries made in wetland sites such as the Somerset levels and around the Humber prompted individual archaeologists to look at peats found on the beaches and seabed (**colour plate 1; colour plate 2**). They found rich evidence of prehistoric landscapes and their inhabitants. Secondly, fierce lobbying by nautical archaeologists won support for shipwrecks to be added to the National Monuments Record. Thirdly, a number of studies and test surveys, notably in the Isles of Scilly, Cleveland, Yorkshire and Gwynedd, proved that the coast was rich not only in prehistoric but in industrial remains and that many many sites were severely threatened by erosion.

These pioneering studies also found a number of problems, both theoretical and logistical. There were three main issues:

1 Setting geographic limits

Defining the length and breadth of the British coast is not simple. There are greater and lesser estimates of its length. Measured on the high tide line it swings into every bay and

8   Seasalter Wreck, Kent. The plundering of old shipwrecks embedded in beaches fuelled the lobby for better care of the underwater heritage which in turn encouraged pioneering surveys of the coast. For some regions the great breadth of the intertidal area is a logistical problem

inlet and reaches deep inside the country to the highest tidal point of rivers, as far inland as London on the Thames for example. On the low tide line it will be much shorter as this cuts across the mouths of many bays and rivers. Even the scale of the map used for measuring will affect the final total. The distance will be shorter when measured on a small-scale map, which smooths into a relatively undeviating line the many small indentations of the coast depicted more clearly on a large-scale map. In addition there is the problem of deciding which islands, islets and rocks to include. Orkney, for example, has 67 islands, Shetland has more than 100, and the Isles of Scilly have more than 120 islands and tidally uncovered rocks.

The coast is where the land meets the sea but the earth and the water are not separated by a single, narrow line. In the Bristol Channel, for example, the range between high and low tide alone can be measured horizontally in hundreds of metres across gently shelving beaches or mudflats. Instead of a fixed line on a map it is more helpful to think of the Coastal Zone. This comprises the area of land influenced by the sea and the area of the sea influenced by the land. It may stretch far inland across, for example, a broad plain to a natural barrier such as a range of hills. The tide mills at Bromley-by-Bow, for instance, are far from the open coast on a quiet Hertfordshire backwater, The influence of the land may also reach many miles to seaward perhaps to areas where industrial, domestic or military waste has been dumped (**22**).

2 Reconciling today's coast with its predecessors

The present coast is not the coastline known by generations in earlier decades and centuries. Every day the coast is changed, often imperceptibly, by the action of wind, rain, rivers and sea. Parts of Yorkshire and Suffolk are losing several feet of coastal land annually through erosion. Sometimes a single cliff fall is awesome in its size and visual impact (**9**). In August 1999, national headlines reported a 200yd long stretch of the famous Beachy Head, East Sussex, crashing to the shore below. Occasionally dramatic change is wrought by extreme weather and storm surges. The tragic flooding around Towyn on Kinmel Bay, Clwyd, in 1991 was perhaps similar to that experienced by Hayling Island, Hampshire, in 1324. On that occasion the sea never withdrew and the islanders lost land and even the church of St Swithun.

Tracing the shape of the coast through old maps and documents shows that sometimes it is the land rather than the sea which advances. During the last century the growth of marsh narrowed the shallow, sandy Dee Estuary and left Neston and then Parkgate, Cheshire, inaccessible to ships. Slowly growing sand and shingle spits have similarly changed river mouths. In West Sussex the new port of Shoreham replaced Old Shoreham which had once traded at the river mouth. Cataclysmic changes can also cause the coast to advance. In 1720, for example, the harbour of prosperous Rattray, Grampian, was instantly closed when a shingle bank was thrown across the mouth of Loch Strathbeg overnight trapping a ship inside. Rattray itself decayed and the loch remains landlocked.

Engineering can reinforce natural coastal changes. The once wide inlet of the Wash, Norfolk/Lincolnshire, was naturally filled by deposition of marine silts and build up of peats. The pace by which the land advanced was increased by the cutting of drainage ditches and construction of banks against flooding. Dover, Kent, lies on a small river the mouth of which was pushed westward by the build-up of shingle. The construction of buildings consolidated the shingle bank and the artificial harbour lies entirely to seaward. Modern engineering is often designed to impede natural coastal change. The Isle of Wight Council, for example, is planning to change the configuration of the coast by infilling a small bay so as to control slumping cliffs.

Coastal change over thousands of years is even more complex. Global warming and sea level rise are now a household topic and the potential for low-lying areas to be lost is readily understood. Similar marine inundation caused the coastline of Britain to retreat as the sea gradually flooded areas such as the southern North Sea, the Solent, the coast of Cornwall, and the Bristol Channel.

The lateral position of the coast depends not only on the level of the sea but on the relative height of the land. The massive ice-sheets had depressed the land and when their weight was removed land masses, such as Scotland, actually began rising, so that former beaches (for example on Arran) now stand far above today's sea level. The uplift of some areas continues to create down-warping in others; rather like bending a sheet of plastic, South-east England is forced down as Scotland rises. The effects of rising sea level are more readily seen in those areas experiencing down-warping. Studies of sea level since the last Ice Age have not plotted a steady and continuous rise. There have been fluctuations, showing that the changes and the relative height of the sea to the land can vary within quite small areas and that local conditions, such as weather, can have an important affect.

3 Understanding multiple environments

The coast comprises many diverse environments; each of which has the potential to preserve remains from the past. These environments present different logistical problems for archaeological teams.

When studying the past the urban coast is far from barren. Structures such as warehouses and docks, harbour lights and piers have long working lives and are often still in use. Some have been redeveloped and given modern uses but their design and architectural features betray their origins. The construction of riverfronts, especially in the Victorian era, sealed older port facilities behind and beneath stone quays. This has protected them from other destructive forces such as tidal erosion. In the twentieth century many urban riverfronts have become redundant and ripe for redevelopment. The Town & Country planning system provides for professional archaeologists to examine structures uncovered during the digging of foundations for modern buildings. Their work is however constrained by the schedules set for construction and by the limited areas available for inspection. Excavations at Kirkwall, Montrose, Newcastle upon Tyne, Hartlepool, London, Dover, Southampton, Poole and Glasgow have revealed sites from the eighteenth century back to at least 1300 BC. They include river walls, jetties, boats, warehouses, docks, shipbuilding facilities and factories producing goods for export.

Like the stone of urban waterfronts, the rocks of cliffs may appear unpromising areas to search for the past. However, cliff faces were ready-made quarries from which the sea provided transport. The scars of quarrying can be found in many places, especially Yorkshire for alum and Dorset for building stone. Elsewhere man-made structures have been cut and built into the cliff-face. In the Pembrokeshire area of Dyfed there are hermits' chapels, for example. Military activity has left remains such as the searchlight positions in the base of the Needles promontory, Isle of Wight. Coastal coal, tin and copper mines were often drained via adits which opened in the cliff-face.

Cliff tops were chosen for many buildings such as lighthouses, Coastguard lookouts and fortifications. Modern engineering has saved buildings such as the Belle Tout Lighthouse by moving it away from the crumbling cliffs of Beachy Head, East Sussex. More ancient cliff top structures have long since decayed or collapsed and only survive either as earthworks or buried remains. If they are completely below ground level they may only become visible as cliff falls cut a 'natural' section through their remains. Sometimes it is only the finds of beachwalkers below which alert anyone to the destruction of a cliff-top site. To collect all the information revealed about one site by repeated cliff falls demands regular visits and rapid recording, even assuming that it is possible to reach the site in safety.

During the last hundred years salt marshes have developed on many parts of the coast. One cause was the colonisation of mudflats by spartina grass. This consolidated the foreshore against wave and tidal erosion and sealed any remains on or under the former intertidal area. In places where much earlier changes in sea level had forced the coast to retreat, the intertidal area contained relict land surfaces, often from prehistoric periods. These were now protected by the salt marshes that grew above them. Today the sea is eroding those marshes, for example in the Severn Estuary, and is revealing the prehistoric remains beneath.

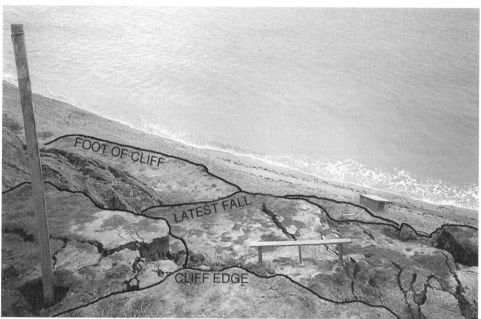

9   Top: *Locals view the latest fall (November 1999) which has claimed a 100 yards of cliff-top path at Atherfield Coastguard Houses, Isle of Wight*
Bottom: *Such slides can reveal buried artefacts but here, rather than scattering on the shore below, they might remain in the slumped areas. The brick lookout lying on the beach is a casualty of earlier slides and shows that strongly bonded structures can survive cliff-falls, if only to then face the destructive force of the sea. No wonder some divers think it is worth searching for medieval city of Dunwich which fell into the sea*

10 Recording the barge Admiral Blake, *Kent. The growth of marshes has engulfed many vessels laid up on the small creeks along rivers such as the Thames & and the Medway*

Salt marshes also contain more modern remains. They have engulfed eighteenth and nineteenth-century wooden coastal and river boats (**10**), of which hundreds were laid up on estuary banks as they became redundant in the face of steamships and road haulage. The commercialisation of recreational boating has sometimes led harbour and river authorities to 'tidy' the banks and these old boats have been broken up or burnt. Such craft were built without paper plans as the knowledge and techniques simply passed from boatbuilder to apprentice. Destruction of the boats also destroys the record of their construction, shape and materials for which there is no other source of information.

Salt marshes have been reduced in size and number by demand for land for agriculture, port facilities, and industrial and residential developments. This threatens both older sites sealed within the marsh and features which were part of the husbandry of the marshes. Around the Solent, for example, there are still remains of structures used for salt making. On the Essex estuaries of the Blackwater and Crouch there are unrivalled remains of decoy ponds used for trapping water birds. Many of these show as areas of differential growth in crops planted on farmland formed by inning and draining the marshes.

Movement of sand and shingle has dramatically changed the coastline and, in many places around the country, has also preserved relicts of past landscapes and coastlines. At Camber, East Sussex, gravel extractors found boat timbers which were probably part of a vessel trapped in the old river when the sea suddenly threw up the ridges of shingle. Sand dunes have often preserved the coastal land over which they built up. Around the country wind and sea erosion of sand dunes on the present coast is revealing sites which became covered at different times. These include Bronze Age burials at Beadnell, Northumberland, medieval villages at Kenfig, Dyfed, Viking buildings in the Outer Hebrides, and Neolithic homes in Orkney.

The erosion of cliffs and sand dunes inevitably scatters artefacts along the adjoining shore. There are also structures to be found on the beaches and between high and low tide. Remains of wooden and stone built fish traps have survived in many places, including the Blackwater Estuary, Essex, and near Tenby in Dyfed. Rocky shores are often mistakenly thought to be too exposed to preserve many remains. This is proved untrue on the Yorkshire coast, for example, where rutways can still be seen and show how loaded carts were drawn across the rock platform to waiting ships. On a larger scale a rock cut channel shows the engineering effort which gave access to the small harbour at Seaton Sluice, Northumberland (**11**). Rock-cut tanks in Fife were used to collect seawater for saltmaking. There are also more recent rock structures, such as the sea bathing pools across the Forth estuary on the Lothian coast. On the beaches, buildings are still in use today. Some are common, like the strings of beach huts which are a hallmark of the British seaside, others are peculiar to individual towns, such as the narrow two-storey netshops used as stores by fishermen at Hastings in East Sussex.

Peat beds are a feature of numerous sandy foreshores around the country. Peat forms as plants die in shallow fresh or brackish water. Since the last century finds of animal bone and flints have suggested the beach peats were very old and they are increasingly being studied as relict landscapes. At Fishbourne, Isle of Wight, individual trees proved to have fallen some 2500 years BC and stake and hurdle structures are equally ancient. Like others around the coast, these enigmatic alignments of stakes may have been boundaries within the salt marshes, revetments against the encroaching sea, or fish traps constructed after the sea had flowed over the old land surface.

The intertidal discoveries have excited interest because they may reveal prehistoric landscapes that were thought to be lost to the sea. As waterlogged sites they contain organic materials such as wood and plant remains that do not survive on many land sites which are literally 'dry'. Archaeological investigations are intensifying on estuaries such as the Forth, Humber, Thames, Solent, Fal, Severn and Solway which are thought most likely to preserve information.

The intertidal zone is no place for time-consuming procedures; work must fit into the few short hours between the outgoing and incoming tides. On the vast and often featureless expanses of mud or sand, satellite positioning systems and computers are used to map discoveries. All equipment must be carried across the often treacherous terrain, or dropped by boats on the falling tide. Any excavation has to be minutely planned so that whatever is uncovered can be fully recorded. The returning tide will either wash away and erase the fragile remains or cover them once more with silt. A mistimed expedition will not only lose information and equipment but could easily risk the lives of team members.

Tell-tale signs tantalise archaeologists with thoughts of what might survive on the seabed. On the Isles of Scilly stone structures can be followed across the beach and into the sea. In the Solent, which was once a river valley, divers have recorded peat at different depths (**colour plate 2**). Cores of the seabed can also be used to plot peat beds. One core

11 Seaton Sluice, Northumberland. The rock cut (centre), whose gates made a tiny floating dock, gave easy access to the river whose natural entrance is to the left of the picture. The cliff top building (far left) is the Volunteer Life Brigade Watch House

taken far out in the North Sea actually contained a flint which had been shaped by a human.

The Hampshire & Wight Trust for Maritime Archaeology has encouraged archaeologists and oceanographers to join forces in studying the ancient Solent River Valley. The involvement of Southampton University enables them to use the most up-to-date marine survey equipment to explore the possibility of locating traces of human activity amidst the relict landscapes beneath the sea. Sport divers join in the work of ground-truthing their surveys since the sophisticated position-fixing systems enable boats to later re-visit the point at which any anomaly was recorded so that a diver can visually inspect the site.

Sport divers have been the prime force in the discovery and investigation of the most commonly known archaeological site of the seabed, shipwrecks. The training offered by the Nautical Archaeology Society has encouraged many to broaden their interests. The Suffolk Underwater Unit, for example, has searched the remains of the great medieval port of Dunwich which was washed into the sea. Meanwhile individuals have tackled projects such as investigating a possible Roman quarry off Selsey, West Sussex.

The *Mary Rose* project demonstrated that the high standards which are routinely expected on land excavations can be achieved in underwater archaeology. While tides, weather and depths restrict working time there are advantages to underwater work. Divers do not have to walk across the site and can position themselves, weightless in the water, above the fragile remains which they are recording. The tide replaces heavy buckets and wheelbarrows to carry spoil from the site. Air-filled bags gently and slowly raise cumbersome objects that on land would require bulky and expensive lifting equipment. For offshore exploration at great depths the limits of diver endurance have already been overcome by remotely operated vehicles and robotics. In the future they will be given the delicacy of touch and their operators sufficient visual contact to mirror the precision of a human hand in underwater excavation.

A view of coastal archaeology

Coastal archaeology may be viewed from a number of perspectives. One perspective sees the coast in terms of environments, at the most simple these are dry land, intertidal and seabed. Each of these breaks down into smaller units such as sand dunes and rock foreshores. The 'wet' environments have led archaeologists to adopt specialist techniques and equipment. Many observers focus on these methods of studying remains, and view archaeology as a series of specialisms; names abound including underwater, shipwreck, maritime and nautical archaeology. To these might be added all the recording techniques such as aerial photography and the scientific analyses such as dendrochronology. The process by which information is recovered, analysed, synthesised and then disseminated offers a second perspective on coastal archaeology. Thus there are two perspectives: one concerned with environments as a source for studying the coast, the other focused on the process of study (**12**). A third perspective views the coast as a subject for study, avoiding chronological or geographic boundaries by looking at individual uses of the coast and sea (**13**).

The coast has always provided a living space made unique by the sea. Coastal communities have become distinct by their life on the water's edge, where they have developed the skills to use the sea. These maritime communities have used the sea to meet both their own needs and those of the inland population. Museums in coastal towns and villages contain multifarious objects, pictures and documents from this maritime past. The artefacts are as diverse as the activities which they represent: from home-made lobster pots to gilt-decorated models of elegant liners; from hand-turned rope-making machines to pneumatic rivetting guns; from racing dinghies to turbine engines.

In 1991, in an effort to understand the value of each museum object, the North of England Museums Service surveyed the maritime collections in their region. The yardstick against which they were placed was a definition of maritime history as 'the use of the sea'. From all the diverse activities the survey identified five principal uses of the coast and sea: extraction of resources, disposal of waste, transport of people and goods, defence and leisure. These uses are supported by activities such as the provision of ports and organisation of life-saving. Each principal use and support activity encompasses many processes, occupations and organisations (**13**).

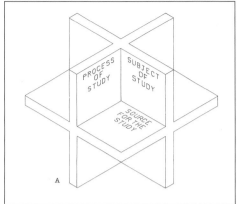

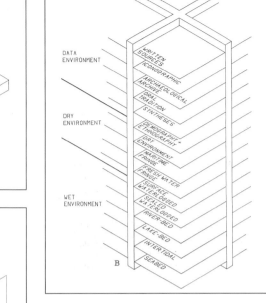

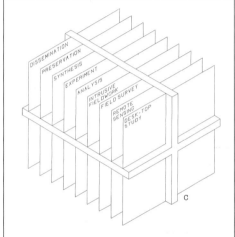

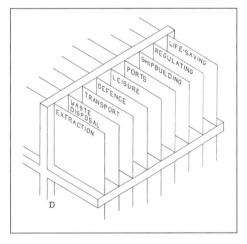

12 *Perspectives on coastal archaeology*

A. *Coastal archaeology can be viewed from three perspectives. Their representation as intersecting planes shows that any element in one plane can contribute to the elements in the other two planes*

B. *Different environments contain the information studied by archaeologists. Here three principal divisions are shown: the data, dry and wet environments. Each is divided into types of environment, which can in turn be split. So the intertidal area might contain rock, sand, shingle and mud areas*

C. *The process of archaeological study is shown here as comprising nine main stages. Each in turn includes many specialist techniques*

D. *The subject of study is the 'Use of the Coast'. Five categories of use are identified: extraction of resources, waste disposal, transport, defence, and leisure. To carry these out support activities have evolved, here shown as ports, shipbuilding, regulating and lifesaving*

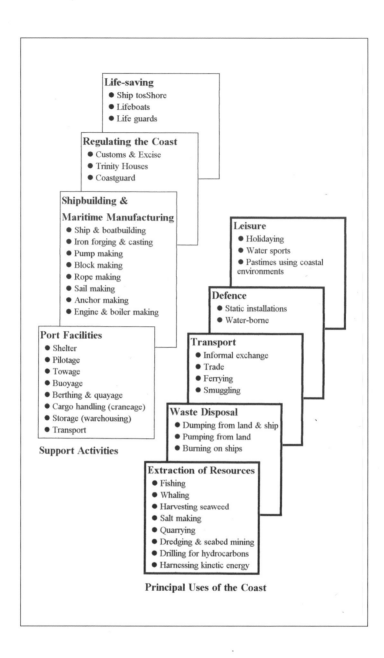

Life-saving
- Ship tosShore
- Lifeboats
- Life guards

Regulating the Coast
- Customs & Excise
- Trinity Houses
- Coastguard

Shipbuilding &

Maritime Manufacturing
- Ship & boatbuilding
- Iron forging & casting
- Pump making
- Block making
- Rope making
- Sail making
- Anchor making
- Engine & boiler making

Leisure
- Holidaying
- Water sports
- Pastimes using coastal environments

Defence
- Static installations
- Water-borne

Port Facilities
- Shelter
- Pilotage
- Towage
- Buoyage
- Berthing & quayage
- Cargo handling (craneage)
- Storage (warehousing)
- Transport

Support Activities

Transport
- Informal exchange
- Trade
- Ferrying
- Smuggling

Waste Disposal
- Dumping from land & ship
- Pumping from land
- Burning on ships

Extraction of Resources
- Fishing
- Whaling
- Harvesting seaweed
- Salt making
- Quarrying
- Dredging & seabed mining
- Drilling for hydrocarbons
- Harnessing kinetic energy

Principal Uses of the Coast

13 The five Principal uses of the coast encompass many operations and processes. They are facilitated by support activities which equally cover the work of many people and organisations, examples of which are shown in the diagram

3 Animal, vegetable and mineral: extracting resources

In their 6000 miles of coastline the people of Britain have inherited their most magnificent natural asset. *AA Book of the Seaside* 1972

Archaeological discoveries show that for thousands of years shellfish, seaweed, fish and sea mammals have been gathered and hunted for food and fertiliser, and coastal rocks and minerals used to make decorative and functional objects. Written history tells of developing manufactories finding new uses for the animal, vegetable and mineral wealth of the coast while expanding technology found mechanisms for extracting these riches from the shore, sea and seabed.

Fishing

From humble Yorkshire beginnings Harry Ramsden has established fish and chips shops across the globe. In prestige developments such as Ocean Village, Southampton, his fish and chip suppers are eaten on the quayside with gulls pecking at tossed chips and binned remains. Fish and chips have long been Britain's favourite fast food with over 24,000 shops open even before the First World War. This modern image hides the importance of fish as a crucial source of protein in earlier centuries and millennia. Too often discarded bones in domestic rubbish are the only record of the tiring and dangerous work of fishermen. Analysis of the species, together with comparison against the habits of modern fish can show whether the fishermen worked on the beach, took boats just offshore, or ventured to deep waters. Without time-consuming archaeological techniques, such as sieving, this vital evidence would be thrown out with the excavation spoil.

A 1950s' survey of fishing in England and Wales separated the complex range of fishing gear into five categories: *manpower instruments* are tools such as spears; *baited traps* include pots and lines (**colour plate 3**); *fixed instruments* are permanent or moveable barriers which trap fish; *drift nets* ensnare fish by their gills and are attached to boats which drift by tide or wind; *drag nets* include seines, dredges and trawls which entrap fish and are pulled by manpower assisted by wind, tide or mechanical aids. These categories could be applied throughout history, and the longevity of some fishing techniques is demonstrated by individual objects found on archaeological excavations. A harpoon and needle from Kent's Cavern in Torquay, Devon, are for example, more than 10,000 years old, while from Whitburn, County Durham, there is a Mesolithic antler harpoon. Iron-Age debris found on Shetland included an antler chafing piece designed to protect the gunwale of a boat from fishing lines. Both hooks and net-making needles were found in Arbeia, the Roman fort at the mouth of the Tyne, while Viking Age net sinkers survive on Shetland and iron fish hooks were discovered beside Hartlepool's medieval harbour.

The importance of fishing to small communities in all eras resonates through the word-picture of life in pre-Second World War Tyneham given by the local writer H. Ashley in *Dorset Coast*. The 12-family village was isolated, without electricity, telephone, mains water or sewer. When mackerel came into Wolbarrow Bay the entire community turned out. As men drew the net-encircled shoal into shallow water the mackerel swirled and leapt. Women rushed into the sea to take the weight while men pulled the ropes, walking from water's edge to the top of the beach then running back to take their place at the net end of the ropes. Such human effort and the catch itself are almost impossible to trace among the physical remains of coastal villages.

Where fish were caught using fixed instruments, commonly known as fish traps or weirs, structures can still be seen on the coast. At the end of the broad sandy beach, which stretches south from Tenby, Dyfed, is a huge spread of boulders and stones on the low tide mark. From the height of Giltar Point this mass appears as a V, its open end to landward while on the ground lines of stakes confirm the configuration. The stakes are only mushy brown stumps but their tips, safe in the sand, are still firm. Nets or wattle panels would have linked the posts. On high tide fish would be carried inside then, as the tide fell, they would be funneled towards a net at the mouth. This fish trap is marked on nineteenth-century Ordnance Survey maps.

Fish traps are also well documented on both sides of the Severn Estuary. Some were built of large funnels woven from withies and laid in rows (**14**). Local names for theses include putts or putchers, and they are mentioned in documentary records as long ago as 946. Construction of the Second Severn Crossing precipitated archaeological investigation of the eroding foreshore which discovered lines of stakes. Many, particularly with a v-alignment, are probably the remains of fishtraps, including a piece of hurdling dated to the tenth century. Similar traps have been recorded on the coasts of Cornwall, Devon and Avon. In Essex aerial photographs have located massive v-shaped alignments of stakes. Some lie beyond present low water mark. This may suggest they are of some antiquity, as studies of the Hullbridge Estuary have confirmed that Neolithic land surfaces lie in the present intertidal zone.

Remains of stone fish traps in North Wales have been linked to local ecclesiastical land holders. All around the country the monastic diet demanded fish. Timber structures revealed at low tide on Fishbourne Beach, Isle of Wight, range from the Neolithic to one tentatively identified as a 'seapond' written about by the medieval monks of nearby Quarr Abbey.

By 1300 English boats were sailing to Iceland where they caught cod on lines carrying many baited hooks. After Cabot's voyage to North America in 1497 ships from south west England began visiting the Newfoundland Banks for cod. In Christian countries, fasting and restricted meat eating had created a market for the dried and salted cod. English monarchs extended these religious practices by instigating fish-eating days to stimulate the fisheries as a source of capable seamen for the navy. No longer feeding only local communities fishing was becoming an industry supplying the growing inland towns.

14 *Fishtrap exhibit at the Wildfowl & Wetland Trust,*
Slimbridge, Gloucestershire.
Left: withies are woven to form a putt.
Right: a fishtrap is constructed between stout timber
posts driven into the ground

The unpredictable habits of fish are an important factor in the success of fisheries. The Scandinavians had the best of early herring fishing until the shoals began using the North Sea. Then Dutchmen perfected well-designed ships called herring busses, drift nets which were ideal in tidal flows over sandbanks, and a reliable system for preserving their catch. The 2000-strong fishing fleet became a foundation of Dutch maritime power. When Cromwell's 1651 Navigation Acts banned imports in foreign ships, including Dutch fish, it gave the home fishing industry a chance to grow by keeping competitors out of the market place.

Great Yarmouth, whose annual Herring Fair had begun before 1240, grew as the main East Coast fishing port. In Scotland a Royal Fishery Company was established at Greenock in 1677. This was soon controlled by Glasgow and the Clyde fishery thrived by supplying the city and exporting fish. The small boats of Highland communities were ill-suited to work offshore. In the nineteenth century as the herring shoals appeared further and further out in the North Sea, ports on Scotland's east coast sent larger boats to join the fishermen from England's East Coast and Cornwall. New railways provided fast transport to the fish markets of inland towns but focused fishing fleets on the small number of ports served by trains. So in the southern North Sea, Great Yarmouth and Lowestoft flourished; in 1899 their respective landings, of 260 and 180 million herring, were enormous. The development of steam drifters, capable of hauling larger nets, vastly increased the catches, reaching 8236 and 5364 million in 1913.

Many local museums have collected fishing equipment which, with objects from fishermen's homes, evoke the era before first steam and then motor-power changed the scale of the fishing industry. Hastings fishermen fiercely defended their right to have stores, or net sheds, on the beach. The pitch-painted wooden buildings are now a hallmark of the old town where tourists wander between gift shops and wet fish stalls. In Seahouses, Northumberland, the fishermen's harbour-side sheds were replaced by uniform, brick lock-ups which offer no such heritage ambience for the passing tourist. However, the local Marine Life Centre and Fishing Museum acquired much of its large and important collection of fishing gear when the old sheds were cleared.

For traditional fishermen a family had always been essential. Children collected shellfish for bait, grandparents baited hooks, wives helped launch boats, gut and sell fish. Scottish women even carried their husbands into the water so they could start the day dry. Cash income depended on selling their fish at nearby towns. Local historians relate how, if the boats were late home, the fishwomen of Musselburgh would make sure of catching buyers by running the five miles to Edinburgh.

Fish were pickled or salted for the family. On a larger scale it was also women's work to preserve the catch for inland and overseas markets. Up to 10,000 women would walk from the Highlands to Wick to gut, salt and pack herring into barrels. Their journey then followed the fleet through the east coast ports to East Anglia. Part of the room over the kitchen, now a shop, at Swallow Fisheries in Seahouses, Northumberland, was used as a dormitory by the herring girls and fish are still cured in their 150-year old pantiled smokehouse. After soaking in brine the fish are put on hooks set in sticks, tenterhooks, which hang on high racks in the stone smokehouse where oak chippings provide the smoke. Each smoker keeps secret his recipe for brine and smoking time.

Pilchards are a sub-tropical relative of the herring which venture as far north as Cornwall. Watchmen called huers spied for the vast shoals moving up the coast. Their lookouts were covered shelters with benches, sometimes attached to a clifftop cottage. The Cornishmen used a seine net, drawn round the shoal by two boats and then closed and hauled inshore. Kept alive in the net the fish were slowly taken out and carried ashore for pickling. They were smoked but Elizabeth I banned the process because the 'fumedos' were exported to her enemies, the Spanish.

Around 1000 fish would be enough to provide a family's winter protein. These could be home-salted in an earthenware vessel called a buzza. The fish for sale went to the pilchard cellars or palaces, which were walled courtyards, open except for short roofs spanning between the walls and internal pillars. The cobbled floor and gutters led to a central barrel which collected salt, oil and blood. Wilkie Collins captured the scene in his *Rambles Beyond Railways* (1851):

> ... a whole congregation of the fair sex, screaming, talking...and working at the same time, round a compact mass of pilchards, which their nimble hands have already built up to a height of three feet, a breadth of more than four, and a length of twenty. Here, we see cronies of sixty and girls of sixteen; the ugly and the lean, the comely and the plump; the sour-tempered and the sweet — all squabbling, singing, jesting, lamenting and shrieking at the very top of their

15 *Longshoreman Jimper Sutton blows life into a fire of oak sawdust as he demonstrates the efficiency of his back-garden smokehouse for small-scale fish preservation*

very shrill voices for 'more fish' and 'more salt'...Never was threepence an hour more joyously and more fairly earned than it is here!

After standing in the salt stack for a month the pilchards were thoroughly washed and packed into large barrels whose weighted lids squeezed out the last liquor. In the later nineteenth century labour costs were reduced by pickling the pilchards in tanks and using screw presses.

The Great Western Railway entered Cornwall in 1859 and drew the pilchard fishery, now swollen by outside boats, to St Ives. By 1870 the industry collapsed as the shoals had declined through over-fishing. While there are records of pilchard cellars being built at Cawsand, Plymouth, in the 1580s, most surviving buildings are eighteenth century or later. In the fishing village of Cadgwith, on Cornwall's Lizard Peninsula, a restaurant today occupies the old pilchard cellar and the huer's house is on the cliff above.

Unlike pilchard and herring, cod is best kept fresh. This bottom-living fish was traditionally caught using hooked lines. Nineteenth-century boats would shoot 16 dozen lines, each 30 fathoms in length and carrying 6000 baited hooks. Although trawl nets (simply large bags with their mouths held open) were introduced to the North Sea in 1774 it was the application of steam-power a hundred years later which enabled boats to pull large trawls over the seabed. The steam trawler fleets concentrated on railway ports that could carry their huge catches, packed freshly in ice, to the buyers. Especially developed by railway companies, Grimsby flourished and by 1919 it had 514 steam trawlers. Its fish dock facilities were expanded to cover 64 acres. Grimsby Docks are now home to England's National Fishing Heritage Centre which traces the story of fishing with imaginative exhibits including reconstructions of the decks and interiors of trawlers.

In addition to carrying away the catch, railways brought coal to power the steam trawlers and drifters. The introduction of motor engines enabled small fishing vessels to use a wide range of ports once again. Road transport also changed the pattern of fisheries. Kinlochbervie, for example, on an isolated stretch of the Highland coast supports a deep sea fishing fleet, and refrigerated articulated lorries await the catch on an otherwise deserted harbour-side.

The system of catch quotas and controversial financial incentives to withdraw boats by rendering them useless has taken the last fishing vessels from many British ports. The loss of the industry is keenly felt by communities whose families are steeped in a fishing tradition, just as pit closures left many coalmining towns bereft. At Newhaven, Lothian, a heritage centre in the old fish market has provided a new focus for the local community's shared links with the past. The Scottish Fisheries Museum keeps practical skills alive as one-time fishing boat masters sail the restored 72ft (22m) fifie *Reaper*. Its buildings in Anstruther hold one of the most poignant settings of any community museum. A small room, whose walls bear modest plaques, is set aside as a quiet place for families and friends to remember those lost at sea.

Water fowling

Large areas of mud flats and wetlands around British estuaries are now protected as feeding grounds for migrating water birds. Since prehistory such arrivals gave coastal villagers the opportunity to put meat on their dinner tables. In the nineteenth century gun punts were used to stealthily approach feeding birds. The gunner would lie flat as he manoeuvred his punt to within 80 yards (73m) of the flock before firing the large-bore shotgun mounted on the decked forward end. Some punts have survived, including examples in Poole Museum and Merseyside Maritime Museum. In the latter there is a punt built as late as 1940, for use on the Dee, which measures 21ft by 3ft 6in with a depth of 1ft 8in (6.4m x 1.1m x 0.49m). Punts are generally painted grey/blue for camouflage, and in addition to short poles for punting close to their prey, they have oars and sails.

Aerial photography in Essex has revealed the remains of decoy ponds. In plan the ponds are roughly circular with a series of curving arms. Nets were set over the arms to form pipes, and fox-like dogs used to lure the birds into them from the main pond (**16**). Such ponds may have been introduced to England from Holland where they are documented from the fifteenth century. Many of the Essex decoys were visible as cropmarks in wartime aerial photographs taken by the RAF but have since been further destroyed by agriculture. Marshhouse Decoy, near Tillingham is one of 15 decoy ponds recorded along the north side of the Blackwater Estuary. The surviving Decoy Books of Tillingham Grange record the numbers of birds taken on the estate in the last decade of

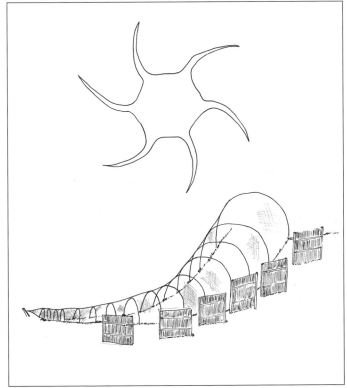

16 Aerial photography has revealed the characteristic star-shaped cropmarks of many infilled decoy ponds. Their overall diameters are around 150m. Ducks follow their predators and so a man concealed by the screens could use a fox-like dog to lure the birds along the net covered pipe

the nineteenth century. Among the outbuildings of many estates were large purpose-built game larders where hundreds of pairs of birds might be hung. A brick-built example survives at Sudbourne near Orford, Suffolk.

The Wildfowl and Wetland Trust now use the restored Berkeley New Decoy in Slimbridge, Gloucestershire to catch birds for ringing and release. The decoy was built in 1843 and in the 1853/4 season trapped 1410 birds for Berkeley Castle. Visitors to Slimbridge can also see the restored stone duck house which was used as a temporary store for the catch.

Whaling

Beach-combing has always been an essential part of life for coastal communities. It regularly provided useful raw materials and always offered the hope of finding something of real value. The occasional stranding of whales was a particular bounty. This is probably the source of the whalebone fashioned objects such as the Viking Age linen smoothers. As the power of English and Scottish monarchs grew they claimed the valuable right to stranded whales. In later centuries the skeletons of stranded whales became visitor attractions. One was placed on Boscombe Pier around 1897 and for many years the entrance to Blackgang Chine, Isle of Wight, was through a whale skeleton, which is still on display.

It is not hard to imagine that it was fishermen in prehistory, perhaps boasting of their skills, who first put off from the shore in small boats to catch a whale. As recently as 1843 the same bravado must have fuelled the ferrymen of Queensferry on the Firth of Forth who claim one of the last recorded whale catches on the Scottish coast, taking over an hour to bring the 51ft (15.5m) long creature ashore. Communities on Shetland, Orkney and the Hebrides followed a Norse tradition of catching schools of pilot whales by driving them onto shallow beaches. Known as a caa this last happened in 1903 on Shetland.

British deep sea whaling was underway by the seventeenth century. Hull sent two boats to the Arctic in 1611 while Nathaniel Udward, for example, was licensed in 1626 to send two whaling ships to fish off Greenland and supply oil for his soapworks in Leith. Whale oil was also used to make paint and putty, and later for street and factory lighting. Pliable whalebone made excellent whips and fishing rods, while the fashion for ladies' bone corsets is said to have doubled the taking of whales. Capital was needed to buy, fit, victual and man large whaling ships. Whaling from British ports only became profitable when import duties raised the price of vegetable and whale oil imported from Europe. British whaling was encouraged from 1733 by a government subsidy, as hardy sailors with experience of 300-400-ton vessels were a useful source of seamen for the Royal Navy. There was a further boom in whaling once the War of American Independence ended supplies of colonial caught whale oil.

Whaling was an opportunity for profit-making in small ports lacking the populous hinterlands, raw materials or manufacturing which sustained larger ports. While London entered the Antarctic whale fishery, Scottish ports including Dunbar, Leith, Aberdeen and Montrose prospered by sending ships to the Arctic. For small ports whaling was a great enterprise; in 1791 with just three of Scotland's 23 whalers, Montrose brought home 28% and 33% of the total oil and bone. In spring, fleets left in gala atmosphere and returned in late summer to rapturous welcome.

Boiling houses, marked by their pungent, oily smell, were the shore-side face of whaling. These opened and closed as whaling companies were created and failed. Townspeople marked the achievement of their whalermen, and the strong-nerved financiers, by setting up arches of whales' jawbones at prominent locations such as the 613ft (187m) high Law at North Berwick, Lothian. Some bones survive in private premises, like Montrose Rope & Sail Works, while towns such as Hull have moved them close to museums (Pickering Park site). At Whitby the whalebone arch which takes pride of place alongside a statue of the port's famous son, Captain Cook, was presented to the town by Thor Heyerdahl in 1963. Most whaling artefacts are confined to museum displays including those at Montrose, Berwick Town Hall, Town Docks Hull, Whitby, and Milford Haven Museum which was built in 1797 as a store for whale oil. The houses of whaling agents, responsible for obtaining crews, are among the historic buildings of Stromness, Orkney.

Kelp burning

In the powerful 1990 film *The Field*, the status and emotions of the central characters pivot on their cultivation of a small piece of barren Irish land. Seaweed, organic and nutrient-filled, carried on their backs from the beach gave fertility to their prized field. On the Atlantic coast of Britain, most notably in the Hebrides, Orkney and the Isles of Scilly, this traditional use of seaweed was replaced in the eighteenth century by a new activity, kelp burning, which produced an instant cash return.

The production of kelp began around 1720 and enjoyed a boom from 1780 as new chemical industries demanded potash and soda. Orkney sent kelp to the glass and soap manufacturers of north east England while the Isles of Scilly supplied the glassmakers of Bristol. The home suppliers profited while first war and then high import duties squeezed out foreign competitors. After 1830 free trade allowed cheap imports of Spanish barilla, made from the cali herb, to flood the market which made British production much less profitable.

Around 3000 Orcadians worked cutting, drying and burning the kelp. Their labour was controlled by lairds who gained cash profits from selling and shipping kelp which formed two-thirds of the islands' exports. Returning ships brought coal to fuel the kilns.

Rock weed was cut with serrated hooks while, mainly in the winter, driftweed or tang was simply collected having washed on to the beaches. The weed was heaped to dry and then burnt in small kilns. On Orkney these were nothing more than a circular pit about 5ft (1.5m) in diameter and 1ft (0.3m) deep, but on Shetland and in the Hebrides kilns were rectangular. Some kilns were lined with flat stones. A small kelp fire was lit in the centre of the kiln and then tang was piled on. The air supply was sometimes controlled by a covering of turves. Kilns burnt for a day before being thoroughly raked. After solidifying for two days the kelp became hard and coarse, with a whitish to grey or dark blue to black appearance. The kilns were then 'raised', whereby the kelp was broken into lumps weighing around 28lb (12.7kg).

While only a dozen kilns or pits have been discovered on the Isles of Scilly, numerous kilns have been located around Orkney, the most accessible are on the foreshore at Elsness in Sanday. Tankerness House Museum in Kirkwall includes kelp-making tools in its exhibits.

Mineral quarrying, dredging, mining and drilling

The recent discovery of the high-value metal platinum on the tiny Scottish island of Rhum has raised hopes that veins of sufficient size for commercial extraction may be found among the igneous rocks of the north west coast. Nothing is new. The exploitation of coastal deposits of minerals can be traced as far back as the first metal-using people. The rocks and deposits in cliffs, beaches, the intertidal area and seabed have all been exploited.

Cliffs offer readily accessible rock exposures while the sea provides relatively easy and cheap transport for heavy, bulky minerals and a place to dump waste. The oldest coastal mines in Britain are copper workings on the Great Orme in Gwynedd. Around 3000 years ago miners used fire and antler picks to win the copper which smiths mixed with tin to create bronze axes and blades (**6**). Written records describe Cornish tin smelted into knuckle-shaped ingots and shipped to supply the Roman Empire. Some 86kg (189lb) of tin ingots found in the Erme Estuary, Devon, possibly date to this time. The later coastal landscape of Cornwall is characterised by the redundant engine houses whose massive beam-engine pumps kept dry the tin and copper mines which supplied the British Empire.

The industrial revolution that promoted Britain's expansion as a maritime power depended on coal. The first coal exported from the Tyne in the fourteenth century was dug directly from cliffs beneath Tynemouth. Later coalmines were inland but accessed sea transport via railways. In the nineteenth century Tyne colliers beating up the coast from London sometimes carried chalk as ballast. This had come directly from the cliffs of Kent and once inside the Tyne could be sold to the glass-makers of South Shields.

Iron was the second great commodity of the industrial revolution. Close to the main Pembrokeshire coalfield, iron ore was cut from the cliffs between Saundersfoot and Amroth. There were about 50 "patches", each worked by two men and served by an individual tramway. The ore was weathered on the beach before being sorted and collected by women and children. Cliff-face iron ore workings also helped Charles Palmer achieve a revolution in nineteenth-century shipbuilding by completing all the processes 'in-house'. Iron furnaces at his South Shields shipyard were supplied by his own ships coming from a tiny harbour on the Yorkshire coast, Port Mulgrave, which was purpose-built in 1857. Here ore was hewn from inside the cliffs and brought through a tunnel to the waiting ships. To the south, between Staithes and Scarborough, richer seams were mined and their ores shipped to the shipbuilders of Tees and Tyne.

From the early seventeenth century the cliffs from Saltburn, Cleveland, to Ravenscar, Yorkshire were lined with alum works. Alum-bearing shales were quarried from the cliffs and piled into 100ft (30m) high mounds which were then burnt. The resulting liquid was boiled and either potash or seaweed added to increase its potassium content, or urine to give ammonium. Alum was used mainly in fixing textile dyes, tanning leather and manufacturing parchment. Alum quarries can still be seen; Peak Alum Works, Ravenscar which operated from 1650-1850 has been opened by the National Trust. On rock foreshores, notably at Ravenscar, Saltwick Bay and Black Nab, industrial archaeologists have traced remains of rutways, where carts were wheeled to loading ships, and of slipways and docks.

17 Cliffs to the west of Durlston Head, Dorset, where small rowing boats loaded stone blocks direct from cliff-face quarries. The importance of local quarrying is marked by a stone globe erected on Durlston Head in 1887 by George Burt, partner of quarryman John Mowlem whose later building firm grew to be MOWLEM construction

Cliff quarries also provided building materials and precious minerals. The Romans chose Bembridge limestone from the Isle of Wight to use in the palace at Fishbourne, Chichester, almost certainly cutting and loading it on the beaches. The shale which they lathe-turned into bracelets and polished with beeswax came from the cliffs in Kimmeridge Bay where nineteenth-century extraction has left the cliff honeycombed with 5000ft (1500m) of tunnels.

Portland Stone was made fashionable by Sir Christopher Wren during the rebuilding of London after the Great Fire of 1666. The scale of quarrying on Portland, Dorset, can be gauged from the huge harbour breakwaters that link the island to the shore. They were built from centuries of quarry waste, stone unsuitable for buildings, which was estimated at some 200 million tons. To the east, near Swanage, deep caves were cut in the cliffs around Durlston Head to supply fleets of ships carrying stone to London (**17**).

On the Cornish coast above Lamorna Cove are three huge granite quarries that ceased work about 1911. From here a 24ft (7.3m) high obelisk weighing 20 tons was taken for display in the 1851 Great Exhibition. Such stone blocks were originally dragged with chains to the Lamorna quay. Later they were shipped from Penzance for prestigious engineering projects such as Admiralty Pier, Dover, the lighthouses of Bishop Rock, Wolf Rock and Longships, and New Scotland Yard. At the other end of the country on the Highland coast is Castleton where a harbour was built to ship sandstone quarried virtually on the shore. Visitors can trace the layout of the works, in which stone was cut by water-powered saws.

Other materials could be collected directly from the beach. At low tide near the mouth of the River Rother, East Sussex, gaff-rigged 'boulder boats' were hand-filled with blue coloured flints. These were destined for the Staffordshire potteries for use as a strengthening agent. Nineteenth-century ships carried away iron stones from the foot of the cliffs forming Hengistbury Head, Dorset. While they left no trace, the removal of stone is thought to have hastened erosion of the headland. This leaves archaeologists to guess at how much more extensive might have been the Iron Age settlement than the remains explored atop the surviving headland.

Sea sand also had its uses. Before burnt lime was available it was spread on fields with broken chalk to improve soil quality. Sand was also sold as ballast for ships. Small Humber sloops would land on sandbanks at low tide and in five or six hours their two-man crew would shovel 40 or 50 tons into the hold. From digging at low tide dredging developed via the use of long-handled scoops rigged over the side of vessels. After 1774 convicts laboured on the Thames with these bag and spoon dredgers. They worked for Trinity House, London, which had the rights to river sand. Large quantities would have filled empty colliers and finished up in the artificial sand hills along the River Tyne.

While dredging was developed to provide sufficient depth of water in harbours and rivers, powered dredgers also enabled the extraction of sand and gravel from the open seabed for engineering projects. The convenience of landing aggregates close to construction sites has meant that many older dredgers remained at work using quays in minor rivers and ports which larger modern vessels could not reach. These facilities can be seen in the rivers of south east England and along the Bristol Channel, their wharves lined with grabs for unloading the aggregates — machinery which is unnecessary for more

18 Loaded with seabed aggregate the suction dredger ARCO Dee *(top)* can slip into the River Rother only on the very top of the tide as the sea crosses the marshes. This picture also shows the hazards of intertidal work: at low water Nautical Archaeology Society volunteers were excavating one of two barges whose gunwales are now just visible on the marsh edgeSeen from above the bridge looking aft, the hold-wide grab of ARCO Dee's self-discharging gear *(middle)* can be compared with the quayside grab being used to unload the smaller Bowcross in the River Medina in 1995 *(bottom)*

sophisticated dredgers that are self-discharging (**18**).

American oil fields were first tapped in the nineteenth century and, like all liquids, this precious commodity was shipped to Britain in barrels. In 1886 the first purpose built oil-tanker was launched by Armstrong Mitchells & Co on the River Tyne. Over the next hundred years the development of these specialist vessels into supertankers spawned oil terminals, with refineries and chemical works, on deep-water estuaries such as Milford Haven and Southampton Water.

The search for hydrocarbon fuels began in the North Sea in 1957. Production of oil and gas started in 1972 and peaked in the 1980s when the United Kingdom had 92 platforms. Generally gas comes from the southern North Sea, in waters usually no more than 50m deep, and was created from coal some 300 million years ago, while oil which was formed some 150 million years ago is found in the deeper waters further north. The massive tubular legs of production rigs stand on the seabed which may be 100m below while their platforms are high above the mighty waves of the North Sea. Pipelines bring oil ashore to Orkney, the Grampian coast and the Tees Estuary. Aberdeen, closer to production sites, has developed to service the offshore industry while on the Tyne, shipbuilding know-how has diversified into constructing elements of oil rigs. The intense environmental debate over decommissioning drilling rigs naturally leads industrial archaeologists to speculate as to what physical evidence will survive of these huge structures once the fossil fuels are exhausted.

Salt extraction

Seawater itself contains minerals. The bricks of older houses in the Lanes of Brighton have a grey or black glossy appearance that was produced by adding seawater during manufacture.

In the centuries before refrigerators and freezers, sea salt was the all-important preservative which kept meat and fish through the lean winter months or long voyages. Around many British estuaries seawater was evaporated to produce salt and, especially on the east coast, this industry can be traced back to at least the Roman period. On the coast of Essex more than 300 'redhills' have been recorded. Their descriptive name refers to low mounds of burnt clay or earth. Many of these include fired clay objects, called briquetage, which are the remains of clay bars used to support pans, or of clay vessels in which seawater was evaporated and salt collected. Redhills have also been found along the Suffolk coast at Blythburgh, Snape, Trimley and Iken.

Salt making takes place at the very edge of the land and the search for traces of early salt production must take account of the position of old coastlines. Redhills in Lincolnshire lie some miles from the sea at the landward edge of the present coastal plain, while elsewhere they have been lost to the sea. Over the centuries such losses will have passed unrecorded, leaving knowledge of salt making biased to surviving sites.

The large number of saltpans listed in the Domesday Book (1086) shows how widespread production was in the eleventh century; they include 22 in Hampshire, at least 61 in Sussex and Kent, 22 in Essex, 10 in Suffolk and 34 in Lincolnshire. By 1743

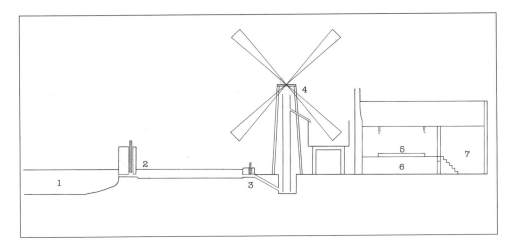

19 Salt extraction

This schematic representation is based on historical accounts of salt extraction at Lymington with
information from the St Monan's excavation used for the boiling house

1 The tide fills a shallow pond
2 Seawater is let via a sluice into the salterns, divided by low banks into ponds of about 20ft (6m)
square
3 After natural evaporation water, the sluice is raised to allow the brine to flow from the saltern
4 A wooden wind engine (12-14ft/3.6-4.3m high) pumps the brine into a cistern
5 The shallow pan (about 8ft/2.4m square) in the low, pitch-roofed boiling house is filled by
gravity. Pulleys and hooks enable the pans to be moved
6 The pan is supported over a coal fire
7 From the adjoining room coal can be fed into the furnace, and a flight of steps leads to the pan

Hampshire had 18 salterns, each with between 1 and 28 boiling pans. Production centred
on the marshes around the Solent where the late eighteenth-century salt exports of
Southampton, Portsmouth and Cowes reached over 200,000 bushels a year. Lymington
alone, producing about 4000 tons a year, paid £50,000 tax on its salt.

Written descriptions suggest that salt production changed little over the centuries (**19**).
During the sixteen week summer season marshes such as those between Lymington and
Hurst Spit, now empty and deserted, were a smoky industrial manufactory. At high tide
seawater flowed into holding ponds. From these it was let into shallow evaporating ponds,
the salterns proper, which were about 20ft (6m) square and separated by low mud banks
some 6ins (15cm) high and just wide enough for a man to walk on. Once natural
evaporation had produced a brine seven times more salty than seawater the liquid was
pumped by windmills through wooden pipes into cisterns. Gravity then carried the liquid
to the boiling pans. From the time of Charles I these were made of rivetted iron and
measured about 8ft (2.4m) square and 8-9ins (20-22cm) deep. The pans were heated over
coal fires in low brick boiling houses with tiled roofs and chimneys.

At the height of production, fleets of vessels sailed from Lymington to Poole where their cargoes of salt were shipped to Newfoundland to preserve fish for the British and Spanish markets. Today Lymington town baths are on the site of the King's Saltern Baths which provided salt-based health cures. From here the coast path towards Keyhaven passes what remains of the industry: stone-lined inlets for barges and a few brick buildings, now re-used by farmers. Elsewhere names such as Saltern School and Old Saltern Golf Club mark the past Solent industry.

Solent salt makers used coal shipped principally from the River Tyne. Similarly Devon producers, who supplied salt for pickling Cornish herring, relied on coal brought across the Bristol Channel from the Welsh coalfields. Further north salt makers lacked the long summer seasons for evaporating seawater. In Cumbria a concentrate for boiling was obtained by leaching from beach sand, while ready supplies of coal enabled one-step evaporation. Close to the Great North East Coalfield, the saltpans in South Shields were described as the largest in Britain, 21ft by 12ft 6in and 14in deep (6.4 x 3.8 x 0.35m). On the north coast of the Firth of Forth at St Monans, Fife, excavation has revealed the remarkably well-preserved St Philips saltworks which was begun in 1772. The works, which can be viewed from a visitor centre, now comprise two seawater reservoirs, or bucket pots, cut into the rock foreshore and linked by a channel. The channel runs to the cliff face where it becomes a tunnel, at the end of which the seawater was raised by a wind-driven pump. Nine panhouses line the cliff-edge where they could be gravity fed with seawater from the wind pump behind, which stands on the higher ground of a raised beach. Together these produced around 430 tons of salt a year and used at least 2580 tons of coal. On the foreshore only structures below the level of the present wave cut platform survive; erosion has removed the walls that once surrounded the bucket pots, for example. Similar works are known to have existed elsewhere on the Forth and Northumberland coast, but no detailed archaeological investigation has taken place; it may be that all traces have been lost to erosion.

Heavy taxation made it difficult for salt makers far from coalfields to remain competitive, and the removal of import duties from foreign salt in 1823 undermined the Scottish industry. By the 1830s production had fallen dramatically in the face of all-year production of mineral or rock salt mined in Cheshire and around the Tees Estuary.

Power generating

Tide-mills

While many coastal facilities such as harbour piers and rock lighthouses are massively constructed to withstand the awesome force of the sea as it batters the exposed coast, in sheltered estuaries much lesser structures have been successfully harnessing the power of the sea since at least the eleventh century.

The Domesday book records a mill at the entrance to the port of Dover. This has been claimed as the earliest specific reference in Britain to a watermill driven not by a stream but by the sea. Tide-mills were built where an estuary could be dammed to form a pond. As the tide rose the sea flowed into the pond through sluice gates in the dam. Once the tide began to ebb the pressure of water closed these gates and the impounded water was

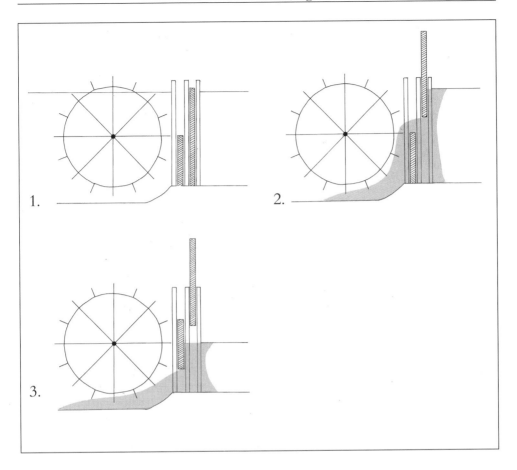

20. *Tidal waterwheels*
1   *At high tide the wheel is stationary and its sluices are shut to impound the water which has flowed into the tide pond via gates in the mill dam*
2   *Once the tide begins to ebb, the water drops sufficiently for the wheel to turn. The first sluice is opened and the water flows out, giving the efficiency of a breastshot waterwheel*
3   *When the water level in the tide pond drops beneath the mid-point of the wheel, the second sluice is opened and operation is now as an undershot waterwheel*
    In some mills the waterwheels are placed at different heights to cope with the changing level in the tide pond

then used to drive the waterwheel of the mill.

The tide guaranteed two periods of around five hours work per day. However as the tides are later each day the poor miller's work pattern also moved and had to accommodate tides late at night and early in the morning. The difference in the height of water in the pond as the tide fell was overcome by either using two wheels or a system of gates so that one wheel worked first as a breast and then as an undershot wheel (**20**).

Tide-mills were most common in the estuaries of Pembrokeshire, Cornwall, Devon,

Hampshire, Isle of Wight, Sussex, Essex and Suffolk. Many of the tide-mills around the Solent were built in the eighteenth century to supply the flour which was essential to feed the hundreds-strong crews of naval ships based on Portsmouth. The visible remains of these mills are varied. The site of East Medina Mills is now a small marina, the mill at Yarmouth, minus wheels and machinery, is converted to a house, while Eling Mill near Southampton has been restored to use. The history of Eling shows how many of these mills had been rebuilt time and time again and that many of their histories, like the lost Dover Mill, can be traced back to the Domesday Book.

The tide-mills often had wharves, adjoining or close by, from which their produce could be loaded into coastal craft. Flour was not the only product; another common milling task was the crushing of bone for fertiliser. One of the mills at Bromley-by-Bow, for instance, was converted from flour milling to distilling in 1727. The diverse uses of tide-power before steam was available is apparent from a tide-driven gunpowder works which was operating on the River Ravensbourne as early as 1554.

Windmills

Windmills could be located in many places but those on the coast could take advantage of the strongest and most regular winds because the surface of the surrounding water provided little friction and no obstructions to the passage of air currents. The section on salt making shows windpower used for pumping rather than milling. The wind-engine at St Philips saltworks was housed in a four-storey tower 7.8m high but the means by which its power was transferred to the pump is not yet known.

In the late twentieth century the pursuit of sustainable energy production has seen the introduction of wind-powered electricity generators, many of which are sited on the coast. In 1982 a three-bladed turbine was placed on Fair Isle then, in 1988, Burgar Hill on Orkney, one of Britain's windiest places, was chosen as a turbine site. Shetland installed a 750 Kw wind turbine with a 45m (147.5ft) diameter rotor in 1988 and a wind farm operates on Anglesey. Industrialised waterfronts are also being used for modern wind generators. Such installations can be seen on the northern shore of the Mersey near Seaforth, and along the pier at Blyth, Northumberland. The Department of Energy had predicted that wind turbines located in shallow coastal waters could generate more than enough energy for Britain's needs.

4 The communal tip: waste disposal

Waste disposal by human beings may be said to have begun when hunters of the earliest Stone Age tossed their gnawed bones over their shoulders.
Jacquetta Hawkes

In 1995 the visiting tall ships brought thousands of Scotsmen and tourists down from Edinburgh to throng the docks of Leith. Beyond the essential ranks of port-a-loos, tucked away from the maritime spectacle was a smart red-hulled vessel, the *Gardy Loo* (**21**). Her name, a Scots corruption of 'gardez l'eau', was once a cry of warning to passers-by when chamber pots were emptied from upper windows onto the eighteenth-century Edinburgh streets. Launched in 1976 as a sewage-sludge dump ship its name boasted the improved methods of waste disposal then enjoyed by the great city. In the 1990s, however, public opinion and international conventions have pressed forward the campaign to cleanse the global seas by introducing alternative methods for waste disposal. These demand extensive engineering works along the coast, where by age-old tradition the waste of the land-dwelling has been cast into the sea.

The earliest inhabitants of the British coast simply walked away from their rubbish problem. With the nomadic lifestyle of Mesolithic hunter-gatherers there was no difficulty in finding another cave or campsite once the odour or flies of their rubbish heaps become unbearable. The people have gone, but where their coastal middens suvive they tell us of their seasonal diet of shellfish. As cultivation introduced a more settled lifestyle, communities were gradually confronted by the accumulation of human, animal and domestic waste literally on their doorsteps. Some 4500 years ago the first settlers on Orkney put kitchen waste to good use, insulating their dry-stone houses against the Atlantic winds by setting them into piles of household rubbish. Waste water or sewage was also managed; a stone-lined drain led from the houses to a pit from which the waste was possibly taken for fertiliser.

The development of towns multiplied the problem of sewage. Excavation of the Roman waterfront in London has revealed carefully planned buildings provided with drains of wood leading to the river. Similar drains have been found in medieval towns. Sanitary arrangements were central to the layout of monastic buildings where water courses were diverted through stone or brick channels to flush communal latrines. The latrines, or garderobes, of medieval castles were built with chutes emptying into the moat, or as at Kidwelly, Dyfed, to the tidal river below.

By the late seventeenth century the human waste of expanding London was held in underfloor cesspits which sometimes overflowed into the houses above. A well-intentioned ban on cesspits simply led to the Thames becoming an open sewer. In the hot

21 MV Gardyloo *(1976), Leith Docks. Sewage Sludge Dump Ship 281 ft 9 in long, 46 ft 7 in breadth, draft 15ft 6in (85.88m x 14.21m, 4.72m), sludge capacity 2515 tons*

summer of 1858 the 'Great Stink' of the Victorian Thames became so unbearable that the windows of the riverside Houses of Parliament were hung with cloths drenched in chloride of lime to combat the stench. With the realisation that diseases such as cholera were water-borne the river was recognised as a health hazard, and the Metropolitan Board of Works was charged with preventing drains discharging into the river. Their engineer Sir Joseph Bazalgette designed an outstanding system, which remains the basis of the capital's sewer complex at the end of the twentieth century.

Beginning in 1859 Bazalgette built five enormous interceptory sewers to collect waste from the existing drains before it reached the river. The Northern Outfall ran parallel to the north bank as far as Barking in Essex and on the other side of the river the Southern Outfall ran to Crossness in Kent. To assist gravity in maintaining the flow there were a series of pumping stations. While the sewers are inaccesssible to the public, surviving pumping stations are visible evidence of Bazalgette's work. The Abbey Mills pumping station at Bromley-by-Bow is known as the 'cathedral of sewage' while that at Greenwich High Road, Deptford is noted for its Italianate architecture. A bust of Bazalgette can be seen on Thames Embankment which he designed to carry the Northern Outfall and to form a solid river bank.

In Brighton it is possible to tour the Victorian sewers (**colour plate 4**). Guides lead overall-clad and rubber-gloved visitors from an entrance under the Palace Pier to a man-hole exit near the Royal Pavilion. This unusual tourist attraction is so popular that early bookings are essential and a visitor centre has been opened.

Low-lying coastal towns relied on pumping stations to discharge sewage into the sea since gravity offered little motive power. This was the case in Victorian Portsmouth which was built on Portsea Island only 12ft (3.6m) above sea level. A pumping station was

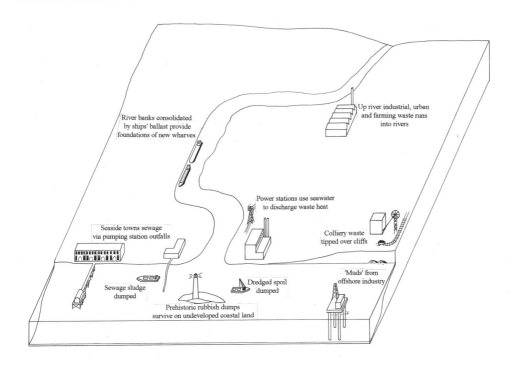

22 At the coast the domestic and industrial waste of the land has traditionally been cast into the sea

opened in 1868 and the James Watt & Co engines, which were installed in 1887, are regularly steamed by Portsmouth Museums at the Eastney Beam Engine House. By 1950 the area was served by 15 pumping stations.

Dumping at sea provided an alternative to sewage outfalls which, were criticised for polluting the sea and beaches. The *Gardy Loo* overcame the problem of eight outfalls discharging along the 10 miles of Edinburgh's shoreline. Sewage sludge was loaded into her two tanks via a smell-free closed system which returned gases ashore for deodorising. She discharged in 30 fathoms of water at two sites 38 and 44 miles off Leith. A larger dumping operation was based on the Clyde where sewage dump ships began work in 1904. One of the Clyde ships the SS *Shieldhall* (1955) is preserved afloat in Southampton from where she regularly steams. A European ban on sewage dumping became effective in 1999, so that *Gardy Loo* and her like have since been decommissioned.

Sewage may still be discharged into the sea after extensive treatment. The upgrading of sewage treatment has meant that many seaside towns have seen engineering schemes to compare with Balzalgette's ideas for London. To ensure clean beaches massive tunnels have been constructed along the length of their seafronts to collect waste water and direct it to treatment plants (**23**). At Hastings a 24ft (7.3m) diameter tunnel is to hold stormwater and prevent its overflow onto beaches. Such underground boring means that these schemes are not confined to dry land, and Portsmouth is being linked to Havant by a tunnel driven under Langstone Harbour. This will carry sewage for treatment and, after

23 Engineering for Waste Water, Brighton 1995. Seaside visitors saw only the iceberg-like tips of huge engineering projects which drove tunnels beneath beaches, promenades and even harbours to intercept waste water and carry it to treatment plants which would then discharge only cleaned waste into the sea

the solids are removed for recycling as organic fertiliser, the safe waste will be discharged from Eastney more than three miles out to sea.

Coastal craft have a history of carrying the waste of urban areas. Whereas it is car exhausts that now pollute the atmosphere the waste product of the horse-drawn age was dung and straw. Barges carried these from London to manure the fields of Kent and East Anglia. Ash from coal fires was similarly taken down the Thames to be used by the brick-makers of Kent. Urine was collected and shipped to the Yorkshire alum works from both London and Hull.

Waste from quarrying and mining has marked the coast. Flooding is a major threat to mining, and adits were dug to provide drainage. The small openings of adits from coal mines can be seen in the low cliffs to the east of Amroth, Dyfed. On the Cornish cliffs the ruined engine houses are monumental reminders of the investment in draining the tin and copper mines, while the cliff-faces below are stained green and red from the ore-carrying water. So great a quantity of metal-bearing water was drained into the sea that in the twentieth century the recovery of tin by dredging sands in the Bristol Channel was an operation worth commercial consideration.

Large quantities of waste have changed the configuration of some coastlines. In the late eighteenth century a Plymouth chemist, William Cookworthy, discovered that kaolin was the principal ingredient of the prized porcelain imported from China. It sparked the commercial exploitation of Cornwall's kaolin, or China clay. To export the deposits around St Austell new harbours were built at Charlestown, Par and Pentewan. The harbour and industrial buildings at Par were constructed on a spit largely composed of sand and mining waste washed downstream. Three reservoirs built in the 1870s to flush the china clay waste clear of Pentewan proved inadequate and the harbour now lies totally silted 400 yards (365m) from the sea.

Just as china clay waste has left lunar-like landscapes round St Austell, so slag heaps are the most usual residue of coal-mining. In County Durham, however, coal waste was also tipped over the cliffs. Though this blackened and disfigured the beaches it apparently also provided a barrier against erosion.

One by-product of shipping, namely ballast, was an enormous headache for harbour and river authorities. Regulation was essential to stop off-loaded gravel ballast forming shoals in Britain's already shallow rivers and discharge was often only permitted at designated ballast quays. The collier fleets of the Tyne had used ballast quays since Cromwell's time. Within a century ballast mounds on the north of the river were over 150ft (46m) high while on the south bank there were 18 huge mounds between Mill Dam, South Shields and Jarrow Lake. With over 900,000 tons of ballast brought into river annually a steam winding engine was built at Willington Ballast Quay in 1802 to haul wagons to the top of the hill so as to discharge away from the river. Empty slate schooners returning in ballast to Porthmadog, Gwynedd, offloaded into the harbour until the site of Rotten Tare was levelled at 18m above low water. A new site was chosen at which so much ballast accumulated that an island formed on which a quay and travelling crane were then built to handle further discharged material.

The revenue from the ballast quays was probably a factor in the Newcastle Commissioners' reluctance to consider an invention by Richard Liddell. Around 1754 he designed a lighter for dumping ballast at sea beyond the 14-fathom line but this was not adopted. Nearly a hundred years later, however, the Commissioners could not prevent a further new invention from making progress. Iron shipbuilders introduced double bottoms and tanks to carry and discharge water ballast thus removing the need for time-consuming loading and unloading of gravel ballast.

In addition to sewage, barges also dumped into the open sea both coal waste and the spoil dredged from harbours and rivers. The seabed is conveniently out of sight and for many years was beyond the type of controls exercised on land. Environmental campaigners have brought to public attention many other forms of sea dumping, some of which are now regulated or banned by international conventions. Oil rigs, for example, lubricate their drill bits with 'muds', oil-based mixtures, which are dumped into the sea. In 1988 they were estimated to have contributed 22,555 tonnes of oil to the pollution of the North Sea. Before 1991 chemicals considered too dangerous for disposal on land were carried to sea and burnt in special incinerator ships discharging toxic gases over the water. Around the British coast there are sea dumps for both military and nuclear waste. The impact of these forms of dumping is measured in environmental change and, in turn, by its impact on coastal industries such as fishing.

Every year the Marine Conservation Society organises a countrywide beach-clean,

24 Industry and conservation are juxtaposed on the modern coast. Power stations dispose of waste heat by using seawater for cooling

when volunteers collect the wood, plastic, rubber and polystyrene which litters the tide line. Such exercises help to quantify the mass of rubbish going into the sea. Not all has come from the land. In 1990 it was estimated that every year 100,000 tonnes of waste came from merchant ships, and fishing vessels dumped three times as much.

International conventions are slowly ending the discharge overboard of everything from sewage and kitchen waste to cargo debris. This age old practice means that traditional anchorages, if they are not dredged or swept clean by the tide, can hold an accumulation of ships' debris from every era. Seabed searchers can find a variety of ancient and interesting objects, sometimes without parallel from the adjacent land. The difficulty lies in understanding them. David Tomalin, an archaeologist who organised an experimental search of the anchorage in Yarmouth Roads, Isle of Wight, concluded that it was like trying to guess what number, size, type and nationality of boats had used the modern harbour during one weekend by examining the content of marina-side bins, but excluding everything which was light enough to float, was edible or likely to decay.

5 People, goods and ideas: transport

There is no doubt that domesticated animals and plants had to be carried by boat from the continent of Europe to the British Isles. Parker Pearson, 1993. *Bronze Age Britain*

Looking for trade

The sea bonds islands with their mainlands, and links continent to continent. The tides, winds and ocean currents combine in great natural transport systems. These carry useful objects such as seaweed, driftwood and even whales freely on to the coast. The ability to construct rafts and boats has enabled seaboard communities to harness the sea as a coastal highway and a bridge between land masses. By the Neolithic period, at the latest, boats were providing contact between the British Isles and the European mainland.

The wake of a passing boat is soon lost in the ever-moving surface of the ocean, yet voyages leave a mark on coastal communities and landscapes. The impact of the people, goods and ideas that were carried can be traced long after the vessels and their crews have disappeared. The landing and processing of cargoes in recent centuries has often left surviving specialist buildings on the coast (**colour plate 5**) while documents can reveal their economic and social importance. The clues to sea transport in prehistory are less clear-cut. While it may be plain that objects have arrived from foreign shores it is rarely possible to quantify the amount of goods being transported or to identify particular people as the traders or shippers.

Cross-channel voyages in the mid-to-late fifth millennium BC are inferred from changes in living practices. New tools and domesticated animals and plants, different breeds from the local wild populations, marked the arrival of 'farming' in the British Isles. Along with the tools, animals and plants came the know-how of cultivation and with it different ideas about social organisation. It is uncertain whether Britain's Mesolithic hunter-gatherers collected 'farming' from across the channel or if Neolithic farmers on the coastal plains of northern Europe moved to this nearby island. There is no doubt, however, that goods and ideas were carried from shore to shore, but the numbers of boats and people making the crossing is unlikely to ever be known.

Beautiful Neolithic axes of polished jadite confirm cross-channel transport. More than 70 axes made from this Swiss alpine rock have been found in the British Isles. These are not everyday tree-felling tools but objects used perhaps for ornament, ritual or as a sign of wealth, so it may be an exaggeration to think in modern terms of a trade in axes; one-off personal gifts or exchanges could account for their presence. Likewise, axes of British rocks are found hundreds of miles from their place of quarrying or manufacture. The thickly wooded landscape would have impeded walking or riding so it is reasonable to envisage transport along the coast, especially as stone analysis has identified quarries at Portland Bill, Dorset, and Land's End, Cornwall, and island linking voyages are confirmed by an axe found in Ireland but made from rock on Arran, Strathclyde.

Debate over the extent and quantity of trade and exchange in prehistory swings back and forth with each artefact that is found at a distance from its place of origin. A single burnt grape pip found at Hambledon Hill, Dorset, raises such speculation. Could it mean that European contacts in the fourth millennium BC were so well established as to bring fruit, albeit perhaps dried as raisins, into Britain; or does it mean that the vine had been introduced as part of the 'farming package'?

Unequivocal evidence for transport by sea comes with the discovery of cargoes. Two seabed discoveries, one at Moor Sand, Devon and the other in Langdon Bay, Dover, have been judged to be Bronze Age cargoes. They consist of tools and weapons made on the continent and, from their broken condition, apparently carried as scrap metal. Nothing survives of the boats and there is no way of telling if they were travelling across the Channel or coastwise. A storm may easily have blown them off course in the way that, much later, historical accounts show ships wrecked far from their intended destination or route.

These two bronze cargoes show the weakness of archaeological information. The 365 bronze artefacts found in Langdon Bay overturned earlier distribution maps, on which so many theories of cultural contact are based. Thinking back to the extent of Neolithic exchange it is clear that all the jadite axes found in Britain equate to no more than a small part of one boat's cargo. As they probably represent many cross-channel and coastal journeys only speculation can tell what other goods were carried, since, being perishable or indistinguishable from local manufactures, they have not been traced amidst the archaeological evidence.

A burial at Punknowle, Dorset, shows that Bronze Age boats were carrying cargoes on short coastal journeys. The burial mound includes a capping of limestone from Bembridge beds on the Isle of Wight. Stone can be cited in each successive period as evidence for coastal transport. This is because quarried stone is both durable and easily recognisable, and petrological analysis can locate the specific origin of the rock. So the Bembridge limestone was carried by the Romans to the palace at Fishbourne; the Normans brought rock from Caen for their cathedrals and the Plantagenets chose Dorset marble for their effigies. Even humble stone artefacts such as hones, quernstones and millstones can all betray coastal trades.

Patterns of trade

Trade with the Roman Empire in tin, slaves and hunting dogs is described in contemporary accounts. Building on such basic information, the complex pattern of trading contact with Europe has been mapped out by studying imported goods, especially pottery, whose place of manufacture can be traced from its design and clay content. The rugged peninsulas of Cornwall and Pembrokeshire were part of Atlantic sea routes with landfalls from Biscay and Cape Finisterre to Ireland and Scotland. South East Britain was linked across the narrow Straits of Dover to Gaul and the Rivers Seine and Somme, while the lands entered by the Thames, Wash and Humber were in easy sailing of Holland where the River Rhine reaches deep into Europe. Much of the trading pattern was a matter of geography, and the natural routes provided by winds, currents and tides; these continued to influence trade as it developed through later periods.

Excavation has shown that the Iron Age settlement on Hengistbury Head, overlooking the anchorage of Christchurch Harbour, developed intensive trade with Gaul from around 100 BC. Its apparent importance as an entrepot only declined in the next century as tribes of Kent forged closer Cross Channel links which ultimately provided a route for the formal Roman invasion. During the occupation, control of the coast became a military concern while on the periphery of the province and after Roman withdrawal, prominent coastal sites such as Tintagel, Cornwall, and Mote of Mark in Dumfries & Galloway provided a focus for foreign trade. Again their role is deduced from, albeit small, quantities of foreign and high-status objects which have been excavated while other coastal sites, with even smaller concentrations of foreign goods, are written into hypotheses of coastwise exchange.

In later centuries the financial and defence concerns of monarchs played a part in shaping the pattern of foreign trade. Shipping became a target for taxation, largely because medieval exports and imports represented excess wealth; cargoes were readily identifiable at the point of lading or discharge, and there was some justification in maritime communities contributing to the upkeep of fleets which would defend them. So that import and export taxes could be collected, legal landing places were designated, with the result that trade concentrated on fewer ports; this encouraged their development of shipping and merchant facilities.

The geographic patterns of trade continued. Medieval ports on the east coast prospered by trading with the powerful Hanseactic merchants and receiving cargoes from Scandinavia, the Baltic and the Low Countries. The trades left their mark through the wealth of merchants who endowed the towns with non-maritime buildings such as the great parish church in Boston, Lincolnshire. South coast ports kept contact across the Channel. Despite luftwaffe bombs obliterating much of ancient Southampton, the excavated cellars of merchant houses have revealed the rich variety of medieval imports. Ports to the west began trading to Iberia and the Mediterannean and in the eighteenth-century Bristol led trade to Africa and across the Atlantic.

Ships and shipwrecks

The prolific records of shipping which abound from the eighteenth century separate foreign and coastal trades. The former were subject to custom duties while the voyages along the coast were not. Some vessels such as East Indiamen were built at great cost for particular foreign trades. The wealth represented by their cargoes meant that the loss of such ships excited a great interest and necessitated costly salvage attempts. The resulting documentation has enabled many of their shipwrecks to be traced and excavated thus producing visible information about the ships and the trades.

Other smaller vessels such as the hoys, snows, brigs and sloops of the eighteenth century were versatile enough to find work in both foreign and coastal voyages. Notes of shipwrecks, such as that kept by Isle of Wight longshoremen James Wheeler for the coast between Blackgang Chine and the Needles, read as a log of these small vessels and their diverse, and less well-documented, trades. Unfortunately, far fewer surviving remains of this type of shipwreck have been discovered.

Some coastal trades such as the carriage of coal from the Tyne were so extensive as to employ whole purpose-built fleets. Yet, until a hull was uncovered by the scouring of sand on a beach at Seaton, near Hartlepool, these too were missing from the archaeological record. The only preserved remains in Britain comprised a section of hull recovered during dredging operations off Rotterdam.

Other craft plied the estuaries and coast transhipping anything off-loaded by the larger ships coming into port from foreign landfalls. Their rigs were designed for handling by few crew, often 'a man and a boy'. Their hulls were suited to the local weather and tidal waters of particular rivers, though a bold owner/master might occasionally cross the Channel or round a promontory such as Land's End to pass between the ports of the Bristol Channel and south Cornwall. Such a topographical barrier usually kept the craft of different coastal areas separate, and so distinct in their build and use. Coastal craft from the eighteenth and nineteenth centuries can be found abandoned along rivers and estuaries. Their build, shape and form have often passed unrecorded, yet many will have characteristics passed through generations of shipbuilders.

Surviving ships and boats can tell much about the nature of transport and trade (**1**). Their hulls can be modelled on computer and analysed for seagoing performance while remains of cargo reveal not only the goods carried but how they were packed and the quantities in which they were transported. Unfortunately the majority of wrecks discovered on the British seabed are relatively modern metal ships. Though parts of wooden ships' hulls dating to as early as the late fifteenth or early sixteenth century have been discovered, they are very few in number. For earlier periods the key discoveries have been made on coastal land. Apart from ritually deposited vessels such as the Saxon oared sailing ship buried at Sutton Hoo, they include the sixteenth-century ship trapped by coastal changes on the River Rother at Rye, the Roman period Black Friars and County Hall ships sealed beneath London as the riverfront was contained by man-made banks, and the Bronze Age Dover boat buried beside a small stream beneath the town.

The only way out is the sea

Sometimes it is not the transported artefacts but the location of raw materials which implies past cargoes. Sea transport was the only sensible means of carriage from quarries such as those cut into the Dorset cliff faces (**17**). Wooden cranes, called whims, lowered huge blocks of stone into purpose-built double-ended rowing boats. With barely any freeboard the boats carried their loads of up to 9 tons to the fleets of ships waiting in

25 Y Borthwen Brickworks, Anglesey. With cliffs and heather-covered hills behind, the products of these kilns could only be transported to market by sea

Swanage Bay. In the eighteenth and nineteenth centuries hundreds of these ships supplied the demand for stone to construct the elegant buildings of London.

London was also the market for Kentish brickworks sited on the clays fringing the Thames Estuary. Sea transport allowed clay to be exploited no matter how far the beds lay from roads. At Elmfield at the entrance to Newtown Estuary, Isle of Wight, there survive parts of a brickworks which similarly could only be reached by boat. On the coast of Anglesey the decaying kilns of a brickworks at Y Borthwen are isolated from any community and its remains include a quay where ships discharged coal and loaded bricks (**25**). Saltmakers on lonely estuaries similarly needed to send their produce to markets and the remains of salt workings near Lymington, Hampshire, include stone-lined docks. Rock cut loading places are found beside Yorkshire alum works.

Consumable cargoes

Unlike stone many cargoes have not survived because they were consumable. Some such as grain, lime and ice may still be traced, however, because specialist facilities were needed for either storing or processing them.

Grain
Far in the north of Roman Britain the garrisons of Hadrian's Wall had to be fed. Grain was shipped up the east coast to mighty granaries whose walls can be seen at Arbeia a Roman

26 Arbeia Roman Fort, South Shields. Mother and son study a model of the supply base with it rows of granaries. These probably received grain shipped up the east coast

fort on high ground at South Shields which overlooks the mouth of the Tyne (**26**).

In many small coastal towns strongly built granaries of the nineteenth century have survived and found re-use long after trade has ceased. Examples can be seen in the narrow streets of Eyemouth, Borders. Increasingly Britain was reliant on grain imported from America. The East Anglian coast became dotted with maltings which, in turn, supplied the breweries of London. A fine example is preserved at Snape, Suffolk, where it houses the concert hall made famous by the Aldeburgh Festival.

Ice

Ice and snow have preserved some remarkably ancient objects including human bodies from prehistory. However cargoes of ice brought to the mild-weathered ports of Britain have literally melted into history. Stone or brick-built stores, or icehouses are the only visible remains of the trade in ice and also of the fish which it was used to preserve before shipment.

Royalists exiled by Cromwell were introduced to frosted luxuries in the courts of Europe. When the English monarchy was restored the returning gentlemen began to build icehouses to cater for their new tastes. By the eighteenth century an icehouse was a common necessity for the domestic management of any great house. They were usually filled seasonally with ice collected locally from ponds and rivers, but these sources could not meet increasing demand. At the beginning of the nineteenth century the confectionery and other trades began using ice. In Disraeli's *Sybil* party-goers enjoyed 'German waters, flavoured with slices of Portugal fruits, and cooled with lumps of

American ice' — ice had become one more commodity delivered by Britain's world-wide trading fleets.

In London in 1830 Cumberland Market had been built with an ice store below, that was 82ft (25m) deep and capable of holding 1500 tons of ice. It was kept full by ships continually ferrying ice from Norway. The American Wenham Lake Ice Company began shipping to England in 1844 but by 1860 Norway was the main supplier. Additionally, the use of ice to pack fish for transport to inland towns and abroad had increased demand in the east coast ports, especially Yarmouth and Lowestoft, which faced across the North Sea to Norway. England was soon receiving 110,000 tons of foreign ice each year.

Icehouses were sturdily built and often partially subterranean. They were usually egg or tunnel shaped and considerable thought was given to drainage and ventilation in their construction. Coastal icehouses still survive in Berwick, Northumberland. The local Tweed salmon dealers first used ice for packing salmon in 1788 and supplemented local ice with imports. The icehouses were built in the 1790s and continued in use to the 1930s. Opposite No 25 Ravensbourne is a pair of barrel-vaulted icehouses with sunken floors measuring 35ft by 20ft (10.6 x 6m). A similarly sized icehouse is on the north side of the river between the old and new road bridges. On the Highland coast a museum now occupies the icehouse built in 1830 to serve the Tugnet salmon fishing. It is semi-subterranean and reputedly the largest industrial ice house in Scotland.

Lime

When Britain was at war with Napoleon's revolutionary France the price of grain rocketed. Landowners chased high profits by bringing as many as two million acres of new land under cultivation. Inspired by recent improvements in agriculture, farmers spread their fields with lime to reduce the soil's acidity and so improve yields. They favoured slaked lime made by adding water to quicklime which had been produced by burning limestone or chalk in a kiln.

A kiln is simply a stone or brick-built chamber, commonly round and bottle or egg-shaped inside. The limestone or chalk is loaded through the open top of the kiln. At the base are openings, draw holes, through which the fire is controlled and the burnt lime is drawn off (**colour plate 6-7**). Intermittent or periodic kilns are loaded, fired and then cooled and emptied. Alternatively kilns can be kept burning, and fed with more material and fuel while the lime is drawn off. These are called continuous, perpetual, running or draw kilns. An average kiln would produce only enough quicklime in one burning to cover 2-5 acres of land.

Lime has been burnt for centuries. Lime mortar was used by the Romans, and later kilns have been excavated in medieval castles. Early details of the construction of a kiln for producing agricultural lime appear in a *Description of Pembrokeshire* 1603. The use of lime mortar increased during the seventeenth century as brick became common, especially for chimneys. The fashion for large houses coupled with agricultural improvement ensured that demand continued to increase.

Most early kilns were temporary, erected to burn lime for specific needs such as building a house. Kilns that survive today are more permanent structures built in the eighteenth and nineteenth centuries. Large numbers of these robust kilns were built

27 Limekilns, Beadnell. A tiny harbour enabled small ships to unload coal to fire this group of four large kilns

alongside creeks and harbours where small coasting vessels could land the limestone and the coal for fuel. It was common for ships to unload onto beaches and for pack animals to carry baskets of stone to the tops of the kilns while farmers could easily cart the product to their fields.

The sound construction of coastal kilns, their remoteness and limited options for re-use has ensured the survival of many examples. They are spread widely around the country. Loch Eriboll lies on the north coast of Highland and has a battery of tall and regularly built kilns on an islet, joined to the shore by a causeway (**colour plate 6-7**). In the small harbour at Solva, Pembrokeshire, a row of six kilns stands at the foot of the cliff, practically on the beach. Coal from South Wales fuelled the lime kilns of Devon and Cornwall while Northumberland farmers benefited from coal shipped from the rivers Tyne and Wear. Beside the tiny harbour at Beadnell, Northumberland, is a complex arrangement of four kilns with multiple draw-holes (**27**). In the 1860s the limestone quarry on Holy Island served a large kiln block which received its coal via a wagonway from ships offloading at the quay.

People on the move

The sea has brought many peoples to the shores of Britain. The marks of individual groups such as Romans, Saxons, Vikings and Normans are in the field systems, roads, territorial divisions, settlements and place-names of the landscape. Immigrants continue to contribute to the ever-changing cultural attributes such as language. While in recent centuries ports handling foreign-going passenger ships have developed distinct facilities, the coast has been marked by the ferrying of passengers since ancient times.

A ferry is best defined as a right to convey persons, goods or vehicles across a river or an arm of the sea. With the right goes an obligation to maintain an adequate service with reasonable tolls. Such services have been provided by boats propelled by oar, wind, tide and engines whether hauling chains or driving either paddles or propellers (**28**). While the origin of many ferries is now obscure most exist by Royal grant or by Act of Parliament. Ferries over rivers and estuaries crucially shortened coastal journeys by land. So Queensferry, over the Forth, was supported by Queen Margaret as she encouraged pilgrims to visit the shrine of St Andrews in Fife. The expansion of road transport has led to bridges supplanting many ferries (**29**), even on the broadest estuaries. The Forth Road Bridge opened in 1962 was then the longest bridge in Britain, its main span of 3300ft (10005m) stretching between two 512ft (156m) high towers.

The sick

Pilgrimage was one of the main reasons for medieval travel. Medieval pilgrims could rely on religious houses for hospitality and many kept infirmaries to care for those who had the misfortune to fall ill on their travels. A young man buried on the Isle of May, Fife, is poignantly marked as such by his pilgrim's badge, a shell, placed in his mouth before interment. As Britain's trade links spread, so did travel associated with her world-wide mercantile empire.

Throughout the eighteenth and nineteenth centuries British merchant fleets carried industrial produce across the world, returning home with raw materials, food stuffs and exotic commodities such as porcelain, spices and silk. The Royal Navy protected this global trade but the price was ships bringing home frightening numbers of sick and injured sailors. The government refused to pay for the construction of Naval hospitals until 1739 when they witnessed the consequences of 15,868 sick and wounded landed mostly at Gosport and Plymouth in just 13 months of war against Spain. Typhus spread from the sick of Plymouth through the country to London, where it killed more than in any year since the Great Plague of 1666. The argument in favour of a purpose-built hospital was clear.

Construction of Haslar Naval Hospital began in 1745. Gosport was chosen as a safe distance from the nearest community but at the mouth of Portsmouth Harbour it was convenient for landing sailors directly from the fleet. The original design accommodated 1500 beds. The building was completed in 1761 and by 1779 housed 2100 patients. The second hospital, Stonehouse, in Plymouth was begun in 1758. Again it had its own jetty which, with the aim of controlling infection, led straight to a bathhouse and clothing store. In 1807 a 300-bed hospital was added at Great Yarmouth.

The Crimean War was the first European conflict brought into British homes by newspaper correspondents including artists and photographers who visited the

28 Kylerhea Ferry. Ferry routes are usually based on ancient rights. Row boats will have operated most routes where now the application of metal hulls and engines has created some highly-individual ferry boats. On this route to Skye the hull supports a turntable-style cardeck

29 Menai Bridge, Anglesey. Bridges replace ancient ferries to turn islands into promontories. The creation of road and rail networks with bridges over major rivers makes modern travellers oblivious to the dependence of earlier generations on boats for coastwise travel

battlefields. Troops besieging Sebastopol suffered appalling conditions and diseases, while the army hospital at Scutari was notorious for its closely packed beds, vermin and over-running sewers. Florence Nightingale's indignation at the conditions won Queen Victoria's support for a hospital in England to receive the wounded of her empire-wide armies.

On May 19 1856 Victoria ceremoniously laid the foundation stone of a new hospital at Netley on Southampton Water. Designed to receive 3000 patients a year the brick-built hospital was nearly a quarter of a mile long. It was demolished in 1966 leaving only its chapel standing in what is the now Royal Victoria Country Park; the present day tranquillity makes it difficult to imagine the hospital in its heyday, with ships unloading patients at the pier, full wards, and field medical staff training in the grounds. The hospital also had its own railway station and electricity generating plant, and, sadly, a cemetery.

Hidden trades

The imposition of taxes on exports and imports spawned smuggling, the trade of goods without paying customs dues. Successful smugglers evaded capture by landing goods on lonely stretches of coast, storing and transporting them unobserved. It was a trade designed to be hidden and leave no trace. There was a geographic pattern. Kent boasts the longest tradition since it was well placed for transporting wool from medieval downland farms. The many coves of Devon and Cornwall were ideal for bringing tea, tobacco, spirits and fine cloth from eighteenth-century France. Scottish smugglers brought salt from Ireland into their country and, before union with England in 1707, carried goods legally imported to Scotland, which did not impose high taxation, coastwise to England.

Some smugglers amassed fortunes by establishing large exchange networks which required the complicity of local communities, though this was sometimes won by demonstrations of gratuitous brutality towards informers. Despite the undoubted criminality of their violence, smugglers have become Robin Hood-like in popular imagery, and it is largely through folklore that their hidden trade is imprinted on the modern coast. Hearsay recalls smugglers' hiding places in caves, country houses, pubs and churchyards. *The Ordnance Survey Guide to Smugglers' Britain* claims no fewer than 250 such sites.

6 Defence and control

> We are used to seeing Britain neatly and accurately depicted on a map separated by the sea from the Continent and with its major lines of communication focusing on London. The vision is one of inward-looking insularity and our experiences tend to reinforce this. Cunliffe, 1995. *Iron Age Britain*

In 1999 private and public commemoration marked the start of the Second World War (1939-45). Anyone who is now only in their sixties lived through the threat of invasion by Germany. During those expectant months political rhetoric and military deployment created 'fortress Britain', an image of such strength that it endures in modern perception of the coast. The military historian Ian Hogg defines a fortress 'as a series of defensive works for the protection of a specific area under a single command'. So 'fortress Britain' conveys two ideas: the first is of unified and centrally directed effort; the second is of a geographic area delimited by the coast, which was the location of the outer ring of defensive works. The image continues to have emotive power with the integrity of the island coastline (notwithstanding the breach made by the Channel Tunnel) safeguarding the separateness and identity of the British.

The image of the coast as a defended frontier is perpetuated by the accessibility and visibility of surviving coastal fortifications, places where families can picnic and play. It is reinforced by the antiquity of the sites themselves. Many of the 1939-45 defences were originally built against the threat of French invasion in the eighteenth and nineteenth centuries, and there are large numbers of much older fortified sites. To understand these it is essential to push aside concepts of 'fortress Britain' and to grasp a mental geography which fits the experience of the people who built them.

The most prominent remains of Iron Age Britain are large and small fortified sites. Some coastal examples are among the most dramatic but their construction does not seem to have been prompted by the threat of a seaborne invader. Allowing for regional variations all the fortifications appear to be the product of internal social changes. Central and southern England is characterised by hillforts, formed by the construction of banks, ditches and palisades encircling the tops of hills. Excavation has shown the largest to contain settlement areas, roads, storehouses and workshops, while the variety and quantity of artefacts is evidence that they were centres for exchange and for storing surpluses. Their exchange networks reached to the coast, a fact reinforced by the discovery of a ship's anchor and chain at Bulbury Camp, Dorset. Similarly, salt, a coastal manufacture, was carried to Danebury, Hampshire, where excavators found its pottery storage jars. Hillforts are not exclusive to the south; the mighty Traprain Law near Edinburgh dominates the surrounding land while major forts are found along the southern coast of the Forth; the visual impact of ramparts and defences demonstrating their occupants' status, power or control.

In Cornwall, Devon and south west Wales there are fewer hillforts but many so-called cliff castles. These appear to be small homesteads made defensible by constructing ditches and banks across the neck of a promontory. Meanwhile prominent coastal sites, such as Hengistbury Head, Dorset, could control seaborne trade. The longevity of such sites is demonstrated by Cullykhan, on the Moray coast: a late Bronze Age refuge, an Iron Age and then Pictish fort and site for both a medieval castle and eighteenth-century defences.

On the Atlantic coast of Iron Age Scotland defensible homesteads were built of the readily available stone. The most imposing of these are brochs, sturdy circular towers, with staircases and galleries within the thickness of their walls, standing sometimes in excess of 40ft (12m) high (**30**). Although the interior may have provided living space, complexes of ancillary buildings have also been excavated around individual brochs. Understanding the geographic spread, variation in design and changes in use of brochs is made difficult by the long period over which individual examples were occupied. They can contain remains from the mid-first millennium BC through to the Viking Age, a period of some 1500 years.

The Roman invasion of AD 43 was well judged to take control of the south east of England which, since about 100 BC, had developed stronger and stronger trading links with Gaul. The Roman historians relate how the legions which later pushed forward into less welcoming regions proceeded by reducing the major hillforts. In advance of their land campaigns the invaders raised their own coastal fortifications. The invasion bridgehead was on the Wantsum Channel which linked the Thames Estuary to the English Channel and divided today's Thanet from Kent. The Wantsum would allow ships to reach Londinium without rounding the dangerous North Foreland. Forts were built at the northern end, Reculver, and at the southern, Richborough. The construction of a great triumphal arch at Richborough signifies the later role of these forts in marking the supremacy of Rome.

The Roman advance and military domination is marked by the known sites of nearly 300 forts. The most renowned coastal examples are the 10 Saxon Shore Forts, spread between Brancaster, Norfolk, and Portchester Castle in Portsmouth Harbour (**31**). Since eight were newly built in the third century and all were placed under a Count of the Saxon Shore they have traditionally been understood as a system of coast defence against Saxon raiders. An alternative theory suggests that they were to form a stronghold for the usurping emperor Carausius, against imperial forces. Equally, they may not have been coast defences but gateways to the province, protecting naval harbours capable of rapidly disembarking troops to suppress insurrection. The fate of the Saxon Shore Forts has been largely determined by coastal forces. Walton, Essex, has collapsed into the sea while Lympne, Kent, now lies inland since the adjacent harbour has silted up.

The Saxon shore forts were not the only coastally disposed installations of the Roman military. Arbeia on the Tyne (**26**) and Cramond on the Forth were supply bases for military operations north into Scotland. The western end of Hadrian's Wall was guarded by a fort at Bowness-on-Solway while mile castles and turrets extended down the coast, and forts survive at Maryport and Ravensglass. Signal stations have also been found, including Filey

30 Iron Age brochs were defensible towers, probably at the centre of small coastal homesteads. Left: entrance path and doorway near Dunrobin. Grassed over remains can conceal ancilliary buildings, perhaps dwellings, stores or workshops. Right: walls survive up to 40 ft (12m) high, here in Glen Beag collapse has revealed the internal stairways and galleries

and Scarborough, Yorkshire; remains have also been excavated on Steep Holm in the Bristol Channel. To what extent northerly shore stations worked in concert with Roman merchant and naval ships is not known for certain. The fleet, *Classis Britannica*, was probably based on a now lost harbour at Dover and a circumnavigation of the islands was recorded by contemporary historians.

When the legions withdrew, the Romanised regions of Britain lost their military defence; deprived of central political and economic control they might once again fragment under tribal or regional leaders. The Roman military structure had in fact never encompassed the far north where, on the Atlantic coast of Scotland brochs remained as defensible homesteads and symbols of power. From the eighth century their occupants faced raiders crossing from Norway in fast sailing ships. Place-names show the extent to which raiders became settlers in Shetland, Orkney and the Outer Hebrides, and drew the islands into Scandinavia's maritime sphere with ships trading to Iberia and beyond.

The Vikings also threatened southern England where King Alfred is credited with urging coastal towns to raise defences. These were not military bases but banks and ditches built to defend individual towns against seaborne raiders. The walled town of Wareham at the head of Poole Harbour was originally defended in this way. Whereas such

*31 Portchester Castle. Lapped by the waters of Portsmouth Harbour this is the best preserved
of the Roman Saxon Shore Forts. In the background is Portsdown Hill where artillery forts
were sited in the 1860s to prevent any invading army from bombarding the naval port from
its landward side*

piecemeal fortifications might deter sporadic raids they offered no defence against a
determined invader. Thus in 1066 King Harold could only oppose the invading forces of
first Norway and then Normandy by personally accompanying his army on the fast march
from one end of the country to the other.

William's invasion force combined the skills of knights, who were experienced
cavalrymen, with a knowledge of castle building. The first castles were rapidly built by
throwing up a circular earth mound, where possible using a small hill as the base, and
topping it with a wooden palisade. Adjoining the mound, or motte, a larger area known as
the bailey was then enclosed by a ditch and palisade. William consolidated control of the
country and people by allotting lands to his loyal knights. Using their personal wealth,
they built castles and, as they replaced timber with stone, developed imposing fortresses
which marked the authority of their occupants.

Early castles were concerned more with subjugation of local people than facing
seaborne attackers. Before the development of cannon there were few ways to reduce a
masonry castle: attackers might force the gates, undermine and collapse the walls, or climb
over the defences. Successive builders incorporated features to make their castles
impregnable. Tall walls could only be scaled by long ladders or construction of scaffolds

or wheeled towers. Parapets gave a firm platform from which archers could fire, while battlements protected them. Gatehouses became elaborate structures including drawbridges, portcullises, and murder holes through which missiles were hurled on those below. Towers, first square and then round, allowed the archers to fire along the walls at anyone erecting ladders. Thick bases made the walls less liable to collapse if they were undermined. In time castles became yet more complex; the strongly built keep was enlarged to contain accommodation and storage, while long curtain walls enclosed extensive areas.

Coastal castles such as Dover, Kent, and Orford, Suffolk, had the added importance of ensuring control over vital ports and rivers and their construction was supported by the royal finances. Whereas south-east England was quickly subdued, 200 years later Norman control had not been fully imposed on Wales. Edward I underpinned his campaign against the Welsh by constructing a series of castles along the coast. While their purpose was to control the land the castles could depend on the sea for supplies. A channel was cut to Rhuddlan to allow ships to lie beneath the bailey; Caernarfon lies on the quay with a sea gate; the later Beaumaris was given a defended dock which could take a ship of 40 tons. The highlands were similarly difficult for the Normans to dominate and their castles are found mainly in south-east Scotland. Some later castles occupy prominent coastal sites further north (**colour plate 8**) but the outlying islands of Orkney and Shetland remained under the King of Norway until the 1460s.

In the fourteenth century, as links with France deteriorated into hostility, towns on the south coast of England again required defence against raids. Town walls began to incorporate many of the features developed in castle building. Southampton city walls are among the most extensive to survive (**32**). These include the massive northern gatehouse known as the Bargate, along with towers and lengths of wall. In other towns, such as Broadstairs and Rye, the strongly built gateways are the main surviving feature. Norman castles and later town walls also fortified east-coast river ports against piratical or Scottish raids, and remains survive at Great Yarmouth, Hartlepool and Newcastle upon Tyne.

Early cannon, invented around 1325, were cumbersome and unreliable for battlefields but could be used against a castle. Artillery was also used defensively and what are reputed to be the earliest English gunports, *c*1365, can be seen in a seaward-facing wall of Quarr Abbey on the north coast of the Isle of Wight. In the following centuries the layout and construction of land fortifications changed to combat artillery attack.

Henry VIII took the initiative in employing cannon in coastal castles and created a system of coast defence which stretched from Humbershire to Cornwall. It consisted of specially designed artillery forts capable of all round fire. The first group were completed by 1540 to cover the coast from Kent to Hampshire against French invasion. They were strategically located at vulnerable points of the coast: Deal and Walmer overlooked an anchorage and landing place, Southsea guarded a natural harbour, and naval base; Calshot stood on an estuary (**33**); and East and West Cowes at a river mouth. Their cannon could destroy any ship that was bold enough to attempt a direct bombardment or which tried to gain the shelter of the neighbouring harbour, river or estuary, while their all-round defences would overcome any landing party sent to capture the guns.

Additional forts brought the total to 20, with the most northerly at Hull and the most

32 Southampton City Walls. Fearing French and pirate raids medieval coastal towns built protective walls. Reclamation has left old Southampton surrounded by land but where the sea once lapped the West Quay there are modern representations of ships. A merchant ship lies close to where a storehouse stands within the thickness of the walls, and a partly-built vessel shows how ships were readily constructed on the water's edge

westerly at Pendennis on the Fal Estuary, Cornwall. Although each was individual in layout, there was a common theme in their design. A central cylindrical tower was surrounded by lower, usually rounded bays which housed artillery in vaulted chambers, called casemates. More concentrated fire-power was achieved by mounting cannon on the casemate roofs and light pieces on the tower. This gave a tiered effect like the most advanced warships of the day. The forts could mount heavier cannon than a ship and their gunners had the advantage of taking aim from a stable platform. Many of these squat and solid forts have survived and are open to the public. Deal Castle, which stands on the beach, has the most distinctive design. In plan like a flower, its circular tower has six equal bays around the base, which in turn are surrounded by six larger bays. The outer ring of bays is sufficiently low for the guns of the inner ring to fire overhead.

During Henry's construction programme, improved cannon were already prompting changes in the design of Continental fortifications. Two needs concerned military engineers: to prevent attackers being able to fire along the line of defence, known as 'enfilading', and to be able to fire on the advancing enemy. Bastions, projecting from the main defensive line or wall, answered both needs. In 1558 the defences of Berwick-upon-Tweed were rebuilt with five bastions. Started by the engineer Sir Robert Lee the project

33 Calshot Castle, Hampshire. One of Henry VIII's stout, rounded artillery forts carrying cannon at ground level and on the floors of the central tower. The castle is surrounded by a deep moat despite the sea washing its left-hand side

cost over £125,000 and took more than a decade to complete. Berwick was crucial in any Anglo-Scottish conflict (it changed hands many times), not only as a crossing point on the Tweed but as a base for ships supporting military campaigns. The town walls open onto the quayside and a walk around their tops shows how the bastions gave a clear line of fire on anyone approaching the main wall. Facing in stone enabled the bastions to have nearly vertical sides which would be difficult to scale, while the earth packed behind could both carry heavy artillery pieces and absorb the impact of cannon balls which would shatter masonry walls.

Responsibility for fortifications was changing. Whereas Norman landholders had built their own castles, artillery fortifications were now too costly for individuals and personal strongholds were increasingly out of place in a country unified under the monarch. Defence of the kingdom became more concerned with defence of the coast, although the royal purse did not always stretch far enough. When Elizabeth I faced the threat of Spanish invasion much of the coast was defended only by her father's forts, many of which had been neither maintained nor equipped, let alone modernised. Even if priority had been given earlier to maintaining these fortifications they would still have only defended key points, such as naval bases, and done nothing to prevent landings on any part of the coast. The scurry to defend the coast in the 1580s centred on mobilising the militia supported by trained soldiers and supplying artillery to the most vulnerable counties. The major military force was based on the Thames crossing at Tilbury where the Italian engineer Genebelli advised on a new outer earthwork. Coastal towns were expected to fortify themselves with earthworks and to defend the coast by driving stakes which would deter cavalry and infantry by protruding 8-10in. For the 400th centenary of the Armada in 1988 many beacons were erected and fired to commemorate the system of signals which carried warning of the approaching fleet. Several of these replicas still stand along the coast, though the original fire baskets have long since perished.

Following the fortuitous dispersal of the 1588 Armada, raids on the Cornish coast continued to keep the Spanish threat alive. In the 1590s fortifications were improved and extended. The Isle of Wight had proved vulnerable to invasion, and thereby a threat to Portsmouth naval base, so Genebelli added bastions to the medieval works of its central fortress, Carisbrooke Castle. In the Western Approaches the imposing Star Castle was built above the Hugh at St Marys, Isles of Scilly. At Pendennis modern bastions, modelled to the shape of the promontory, were added to the Henrician fort. Improvements to Plymouth's defences had begun in 1585 and a new fort was now added on the Hoe.

The sea and coastal fortifications alone are no defence without an active fleet. In 1667 the Dutch succeeded in sailing up the Thames Estuary and attacking the English fleet while it was laid up in the River Medway. The attack showed how easily they might have struck up the Thames at the capital. A Dutch engineer, De Gomme, who was already at work creating a great bastioned citadel above the naval anchorage at Plymouth, was now directed to improve defences on the Thames. His works at Tilbury, comprising six lines of defence, are considered the best surviving example of seventeenth-century fortification in Britain. At both Tilbury and Plymouth the Elizabethan fortifications are concealed within and beneath these seventeenth-century works.

In the late 1670s the imagination and tenacity of Charles II and Samuel Pepys, as Secretary of the Navy, laid the foundations of a navy that safeguarded the English coast until long after the Battle of Trafalgar (1805). They persuaded parliament to build 20 ships whose size and proportions set the pattern for later fleets. For much of the eighteenth century England was at war but her strategy prevented any European adversary from launching a large scale attack on the coast. This was achieved by supporting the military campaigns of allies on the Continent and keeping control of the seas. The skill of naval officers perfected the 'close blockade', in which fleets stayed permanently at sea to patrol the enemy coast so as to impede commerce and to prevent their fighting ships leaving port.

When Napoleon achieved military dominance across Europe the threat of invasion was great enough to prompt expenditure on coast defences. The new defences were influenced by a remarkable fight in 1794, when English naval ships had struggled to stop the guns of the Corsican Torre di Mortella, hence the anglicised Martello tower. The proposal was unusual in planning to cover whole stretches of coast with Martello towers spaced only 500-600 yd (450-550m) apart. By 1808 a string of 74 stout, oval towers had been built along the 50 miles of coast facing France, between Eastbourne and Folkestone.

34 Hexagonal concrete pillbox. Many pillboxes were intended to slow an invader's advance by controlling roadways. This one stands at the end of a causeway across the Yar Estuary, Isle of Wight. The interior is cramped by a central pillar of concrete supporting the low roof

They were designed to house 30 men drilled in the use of a 24lb artillery piece mounted on the roof. The towers stood 30ft (9.1m) high with a 13ft (3.9m) internal diameter tapering to 6ft (1.8m) at the parapet. Their immense walls and ceiling, 13ft and 10ft (3.9 and 3m) thick, were designed to withstand bombardment from ships. By 1829 there were 103 Martello towers; the main line had been extended to East Anglia but individual towers were as far flung as Orkney and the Channel Islands.

Whereas more rapidly constructed batteries have disappeared, over 40 examples of the robust Martello towers had survived into the late 1970s. Other surviving fortifications include the massive works on the Western Heights at Dover, which included underground barracks, and alterations to Dover Castle. The Royal Military Canal still delineates the landward edge of the coast from Hythe to Rye where it was cut between 1804 and 1806 to provide a defensible barrier to invasion and, incidentally, transport for troops.

In 1855 the French forces in the Black Sea demonstrated the inadequacy of existing coast defences by so devastating Kinburn Fort that its defenders crowded into the deep casemates for protection. The destruction was wrought by three small ships whose iron-cladding enabled them to hold station despite heavy bombardment from the defending fort. With the French building full-size warships with iron plating it was time to re-think

Britain's coast defences. Although in 1860 a Royal Commission recommended spending £11 million, work was delayed for experiments and trials on armour plating.

Designers returned to casemates where thick walls and ceilings protected gun crews. Iron plates, sandwiching an elastic filling of wood or asphalt, were used to reduce the opening through which the gun's muzzle protruded. Examples of these can be seen at Fort Bovisand which defended Plymouth Sound and at Hurst Castle, originally built by Henry VIII, which defends the western entrance to the Solent. Focused around the naval bases of Chatham, Portsmouth, Plymouth and Milford Haven the new defences comprised some 74 forts formed from lines of casemates. The impossibility of securing every inch of the coast against invasion was acknowledged in these new defences. Five forts along Portsdown Hill faced north to prevent an invading army gaining the heights above Portsmouth and shelling the City and naval base from the landward side.

Plymouth Sound, Spithead anchorage in the Solent and Portland Harbour were too vast to protect from the shore alone. Forts in the sea itself were the answer. At Spithead a shoal was used to build Horse Sand Fort which was completely armoured to take the full force of close-range bombardment from warships. It was constructed by sinking masonry some 53ft (16.2m) high into the sand to form a base 231ft (70.4m) in diameter. This was filled with stone and then clay and shingle and finally topped in concrete. A 100ft diameter wall was added of granite and portland stone, 16ft high and 14ft 6in wide (30.5m x 4.9m x 4.4m), on which was set an iron ring 3ft (0.9m) wide. This carried a framework of iron girders and steel casings, which was erected around a central tower of masonry. The armour plating was finally bolted on to the outside, and the top protected by thick concrete.

These new and costly fortifications have earned the name Palmerston's Follies because the French invasion never came. From the mid century, however, public anxiety increased over the possibility of raids on the major mercantile ports. The problem was examined in 1882 by the Morley Committee which expressed particular concern for the east coast ports. Nevertheless, forty years later, in 1915, the nation was shocked by the German navy's bombardment of Hartlepool, Whitby and Scarborough and this prompted the construction of new coastal batteries.

Air power and submarines were two of the new phenomena of the First World War. The short range of aeroplanes meant that most airfields were located in the south east. The Royal Naval Air Service opened a base for seaplanes in Southampton Water. Its hangars are now part of Calshot Activity Centre and a seaplane still flew from the site until a fatal accident in 1998. Anti-aircraft guns were incorporated into naval base defences; one of the first of these was installed at the Needles Battery, Isle of Wight. Minefields in the North Sea formed a barrier to German ships and especially submarines. Old mines were once a common feature of seaside promenades where they stood as collecting boxes for seamen's charities. The Nab Tower, off Bembridge, Isle of Wight, which is visible from the shore, is an unusual relic of mine warfare. One of five towers built at Shoreham, to be towed to sea as a supplement to the minefields, it is now a navigation aid in the eastern approaches to the Solent where it was positioned by Trinity House.

Invasion was again imminent after the evacuation of Dunkirk in June 1940. Emergency coast-defence batteries were placed around the whole of the British coast.

These usually had two ex-naval 6-inch guns protected from aerial fire by brick and concrete. The gunners were aided by two search lights and an observation post. The position was completed by shelters, magazine and an engine-house to power the lights. Inland road blocks and stop lines were intended to slow down any advance while reserves moved to a defensive line covering London and the Midlands. As the German offensive switched to their eastern front and more anti-tank obstacles became available, the defensive strategy changed focus. The coast was to have a light line of defence which would delay any invasionary force while the main resistance was to come from a rapidly deployed mobile reserve. Consequently, in 1943, the coast batteries were reduced from over 300 to leave 260 in operation with 70 of these manned by the Home Guard.

Besides the batteries the coast was defended by physical obstacles including seventy miles of coastline in which scaffolding was placed in the intertidal zone and armed with mines. Elsewhere the beaches were mined and anti-tank trenches cut or obstacles positioned. Little of these defences remain, since after the war the beaches were cleared and any remaining metalwork has been destroyed by the sea. However, rows of anti-tank blocks can be seen at Eastney and Milford, Hampshire and in Sinclair Bay, Highland. The pillboxes associated with these defences and inland lines have also survived in many places. The most common form of the ten official designs is hexagonal (**34**) but other shapes abound.

7 Leisure and health

I remember the smell of sea and seaweed, wet flesh, wet hair, wet bathing-dresses...the smell of the vinegar on shelled cockles, winkle-smell, shrimp-smell, the dripping-oily back-street winter smell of chips in newspaper....
Dylan Thomas, *Holiday Memory*

The coast is a national playground where facilities for recreation of every sort have multiplied and where new activities are now eagerly introduced to cater for every taste. This mass of recreational opportunities can be traced to an awakening of visits to the coast in the eighteenth century and to the emergence of the British 'seaside holiday' in the nineteenth. The past two centuries of leisure are deeply imprinted on the coast. Leisure demanded the growth of villages into towns and gave them their character expressed in layout and architecture. There are fewer clues to leisure use before the late eighteenth century and most are linked to individual sports, such as golf and yachting.

Today leisure is an economic concept, a matter of consumers and suppliers. The leisure industry provides everything necessary for recreational pursuits from computer games to mountain climbing. Leisure is defined not only in terms of free time but also of disposable income. From this standpoint leisure was only possible from a time when individuals were able to accrue more goods or money than they required for survival. Free time for recreation, however, would have been known to anyone whose day was not totally filled by the routine of acquiring food, warmth and shelter.

Whether prehistoric coastal dwellers enjoyed particular forms of recreation is not known. The difficulty in identifying their pastimes may lie in the fact that work and pleasure are not mutually exclusive. Many modern pastimes, such as archery, fishing, sailing and rowing, were once mechanisms for survival. In recent centuries they have made the transition from commercial activity, through friendly rivalry and competition, to recreation and sport. Unfortunately a utility object, such as a boat or a fish hook, which has survived from the millennia before written records, cannot speak to tell if it were used for pleasure as well as work.

While there are attractions and activities particularly associated with the sea, the coast also sees leisure pursuits which are as much a part of the inland scene. Tradition tells that as great a seafarer as Sir Francis Drake took his leisure at bowls. The history of non-maritime pursuits has been enriched by chance discoveries on the modern coast. A unique collection of 82 chessmen and draughtsmen, carved from walrus ivory in the twelfth century, was found on the Isle of Lewis in 1831, probably when winds whipped away the sand dunes that had engulfed a small stone building at Uig. Tudor board games are among the treasure from the *Mary Rose*. Divers have also found the lead heads of golf clubs amongst the strew of artefacts disgorged by the Dutch East Indiamen, *Kennemerland*, in 1664 as she broke apart on the rocks of Out Skerries, Shetland.

Golf

In 1457 King James II of Scotland banned golf because it distracted his subjects from practising archery, a pursuit essential to national security. How long the game had gripped the Scots is not certain, but it is said to have been popular when St Andrews University was founded in 1413. Golf's homeland was the east coast between Edinburgh and Aberdeen where the sea had receded to leave linksland, sand dunes covered by thin topsoil. This was poor grazing for livestock but attracted rabbits and the resulting sward was ideal for golf, as it would be for archery butts, bowls or football. The earliest balls may well have been rounded stones gathered from the shore. Early golf links are documented at Leith where the first organised competition on record took place in 1744. The nineteenth-century boom in golf has been attributed to the invention of cheaper balls made of gutta percha, and to the building of railways which allowed more people to use the links. The number of clubs in Britain rose from some 60 in 1880 to 387 in 1890 and reached 2330 in 1900. The oldest surviving English course is Westward Ho! which was laid out in 1864. The competing seaside towns were soon opening links to attract new visitors.

Rowing

Oared boats were the mainstay of commercial and naval life, essential for moving goods from shore-to-ship and ship-to-ship. They were also the taxis of the tideway; on the Thames, for example, they ferried people between the centres of politics at Westminster, of commerce in The City and of the Navy at Greenwich and Deptford. In private hands they became a status symbol:

> The *Triumph's* barge was painted primrose yellow picked out in black, and so were the oarblades; her crew wore primrose coloured jumpers with black neckcloths. As [Captain] Hornblower took his seat . . . he reminded himself gloomily that he had never been able to afford to dress his barge's crew in a fancy rig-out; he always felt sore on the point. C.S Forrester, *Flying Colours*

In place of commercially hired boats, London merchant guilds had their own ornate and liveried barges for ceremonial occasions. These have been suggested as the progenitors of modern racing eights, along with the oared barges of wealthy Georgian gentlemen who might occasionally wager on the performance of their paid crews. The offspring of gentlemen, schoolboys at Westminster and Eton, are credited with nurturing the sport of rowing; Eton holding a regatta as long ago as 1793. From the schools the sport was carried to Cambridge and Oxford, while Durham University had its first regatta in 1834.

Rowing thrived on the rivalry between local working boatmen. Particular challenge races have been recorded such as that in 1866 between the coble men of Staithes and Blyth over a 10-mile course from Staithes to Whitby. Staithes took the £100 prize in 1 hour 25 minutes. With such enthusiasm amateur rowing clubs opened around the country. These included bases on tideways and the open coast, of which examples include: Dover (1846), Folkestone (1852); Tyne (1853) and Whitby (1879).

Competition encouraged experiments in the design of hulls, oars and other equipment. Important designers and boatbuilders, who affected the Oxford/Cambridge Boat Race and influenced the development of world rowing, emerged from the working boatmen of the River Tyne. Henry Clasper, for example, had become a wherryman at the age of 20, and raced locally in working boats. His experiments in the 1840s put him among the claimants to have first introduced the outrigger and his development of this invention enabled him to achieve success by building narrower and longer hulls. Apart from example boats in the collections of Tyne & Wear Museums, and elsewhere, the development of rowing has left little mark on the coastal landscape save the boathouses of still thriving clubs. Henry Clasper, however, can be found by searching out Whickham Church, where his effigy overlooks the Tyne (**35**).

Elsewhere on the coast the tradition of racing working boats has ensured the longevity of otherwise redundant craft. In Cornwall gigs, around 30ft long, were used to put pilots aboard ships and, of course, for smuggling. They are now built especially for racing. Similarly the Atlantic Challenge races revived the building of a type of ship's boat which had survived only in museums.

Yachting

Cowes Regatta ends with a bang as a firework spectacular delights thousands of spectators many of whom get no closer to sailing than the Isle of Wight ferry crossing. The traditional finale sees the Queen's head portrayed in fire. The bond between royalty and yachting is as old as the sport itself. The Dutch literally gave yachting to the English when they presented the 'jacht' *Mary* to Charles II on his restoration to the throne in 1660. She was 52ft x 19ft (15.8m x 5.8m) with a decorated hull and carried around eight guns. She had a large sail area and shallow draught, though a keel was added to make her more manageable in English waters. She has survived as a wreck site comprising scattered guns and small artefacts including fine jewellery. Material from the protected site on the Skerries, Anglesey, can be seen in Merseyside Maritime Museum.

Nearly three centuries after the loss of the *Mary* King George V died and his racing yacht *Britannia* was taken to sea and scuttled. Like the *Mary* her wreck is a unique record of the leisure craft sailed by the wealthy. *Britannia* was one of the large racing yachts built in the 1890s-1930s whose design culminated in the famous J-class whose hulls were 75-87ft long. Costs soared, however, and no J-class yachts were built after 1937.

Between *Mary* and the J-class is a long history of development in yacht building and rigging. Yachting was the sport of the very wealthy, those who could afford to build and crew large vessels. Racing gained in popularity in the late eighteenth century as owners issued challenges against all-comers and backed their yachts with a stake, often of over

35 Henry Clasper, Whickham. With the exception of clubhouses, physical evidence of coastal leisure activities is difficult to trace. The recognition by his contemporaries of Clasper's excellence as an oarsman and boatbuilder has left a near life-size image of the man

£100. Yacht owners formed clubs to organise races and regattas. The Royal Thames Yacht Club is the descendant of the 'Cumberland Fleet', formed by the Duke of Cumberland in 1785. The Yacht Club at Cowes was formed in 1815 and became the Royal Yacht Squadron in 1833. The Royal Corinthian Yacht Club (1872) was formed exclusively for members who sailed their own yachts without a paid skipper. The Corinthian and other clubs began organising races for yachts of varying sizes. In the twentieth century one-design classes were introduced in which the helmsmen raced boats all built to the same design and dimensions. This opened competitive sailing to those with much smaller budgets.

After the First World War dinghy racing became increasingly popular. It was a cheap alternative to yacht ownership but offered the thrill and challenge of high-speed sailing. This was encouraged by the introduction of new racing classes, the International 14-ft and National 12-ft. These are development classes whereby designers continually improve the performance by changing hull features and materials while remaining within certain specifications. The number of dinghy classes in Britain rose to over 300.

The history of sailing is preserved in surviving vessels, wrecks, museum exhibits and those boats still sailed for pleasure. The clubs themselves hold unrivalled collections of models, paintings, and memorabilia recording their members, races and individual yachts. Older clubs with a long sense of tradition have preserved elements of other coastal activities. The Royal Yacht Squadron is housed in a building whose core is a sixteenth-century fort; Erith Yacht Club was once located in Lightvessel No.44 built in 1869; in Blyth the Royal Northumberland Yacht Club occupies a nineteenth-century lightship (**36**), and the Royal Dorset Yacht Club, Weymouth, used a former seamen's home.

Marinas

The late twentieth-century upsurge in' sailing, which includes motorboat cruising, has brought a new form of development: the marina. This combines moorings with shoreside facilities for yachtsmen such as changing rooms, chandlers, boat repairs and food shops. Hythe Marina, for example, was built between 1985 and 1988 to provide 225 houses and 275 berths (**colour plate 11**). Its three basins, served by a tidal lock, were constructed on the mudflats flanking Southampton Water.

The capital costs of engineering pushed entrepreneurs to widen their visions of marinas as leisure providers. Restaurants, shopping complexes and entertainment such as multi-screen cinemas offer the yachtsmen bad-weather alternatives and attract non-seagoing visitors. Brighton Marina is such an entrepreneurial dream. On the open Channel coast its breakwaters, 630m and 1220m long, create a harbour where none existed before. Of the 126 acres (51ha) enclosed, 35 acres (14ha) have been turned into dry land for shops, houses, car and entertainment.

For success, the leisure marina must be within easy distance of major urban populations. A 1974 survey showed that of 48 marinas only 8 were outside the south east, while 23 were ranged along the coast of Hampshire and Dorset. Port Solent is within an hour and half of London and between Southampton and Portsmouth (**37**). It can accommodate at least 3000 cars while overflow 'fields' were able to cater for a massive park-and-ride when Portsmouth hosted the Festival of the Sea. The Renaissance of Hartlepool Docks Project (**colour plate 14**) has included a marina and allowed similar provision for car parking. Elsewhere the conversion of old docks to marinas, such as St Katharine's in London, lack car parking space but their urban locations are served by public transport.

The reuse of old docks for marinas helps preserve some of their features such as quayside equipment, especially mooring bollards. While some architects have warned against the use of maritime motifs some marinas have re-used maritime objects, such as buoys for signage. Marina architects have faced the same challenge as builders in history and their tall, narrow houses lining the quays are reminiscent of medieval ports where each merchant struggled to maximise his floor area on a short length of the prized waterfront.

36 Redundant light ships have fared well in finding new owners and uses. Leisure organisations have played a role in this. Top left: a nineteenth-century wooden light vessel is home to the Royal Northumberland Yacht Club. middle left: Haslar Marina using a lightship in new livery. Bottom left: Spurn (1927) saved as a floating museum in Hull but now closed. Bottom right: lantern of the North Carr (1933) which is moored in Dundee

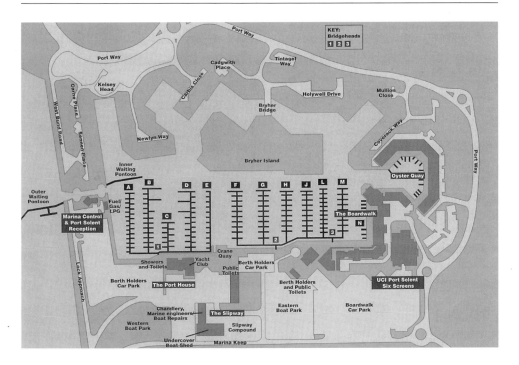

37 *Port Solent Marina, Hampshire. While enclosed docks and their entrance locks became prohibitively small for commercial shipping they are ideal for modern leisure craft and their owners. Islands, piers and jetties all increase the amount of waterfront per acre thus maximising berths and attractive house sites. Car parking, cinemas and shopping areas all increase visitor numbers*

The seaside holiday

In tracking down the origins of the seaside holiday historians are dependent on early resort guides and local newspapers. These are far from impartial in their claims for the 'earliest', 'biggest' or 'grandest' facilities. It is certain, however, that resorts started life as seaside spas, offering cures and later social pleasures similar to those found at inland towns such as Bath, Cheltenham or Leamington.

Scarborough owes its beginnings to a cliff-base spring whose health-giving water was discovered as early as 1628 by Mrs Elizabeth Farrer. In the following century the expediency of drinking and bathing in seawater was advocated, most notably by Dr Richard Russell of Brighton. The pursuit of health was of course a matter of wealth and leisure. The coast attracted those from higher social ranks and its popularity was promoted by flaunting links with royalty. George III bathed at Weymouth in 1789 and remained a regular visitor until 1805. The Prince Regent, who would later build the lavish Royal Pavilion, was introduced to the seaside by his uncle who was a regular visitor to the then undeveloped Brighton. Half a century later Queen Victoria's purchase of Osborne House, East Cowes, provided a boost to the resorts of the Isle of Wight.

Much has been written on the changing social mores of seabathing, from nudity to dignity-preserving costumes, through bikinis to topless sunbathing. Journalists and authors, illustrators and photographers have recorded beach activities, and captured characters such as Mary Wheatland of Bognor and Martha Gunn of Brighton. These ladies were 'dippers', who assisted their clients to plunge into the winter sea. The essential accessory of dipping was the bathing machine, and some of these have survived. The most easily found are those of royalty; the bathing machine of Queen Victoria stands in the grounds of Osborne House and that reputedly used by George III is in the Time Walk, Brewer's Quay, Weymouth. Other beach activities have passed without leaving any physical traces

Once seawater had been pronounced as a cure-all, the coast had a commodity which no inland town could match. With seaside visits endorsed by royalty, the way was open for speculators to turn fishing villages into resort towns. Bognor, for example, was largely the work of Richard Hotham, a London hatter. Bournemouth was created by Captain Tregonwell who purchased land and built a small number of exclusive villas. The well-to-do of the early nineteenth century expected to rent a house or villa for their time on the coast. In addition to sea bathing the resorts soon offered other genteel attractions such as libraries and reading rooms.

The construction of a promenade according to the seaside enthusiast Kenneth Lindley 'was the first step in the transformation of a stretch of coastline into a resort'. Promenading was controlled by the unwritten etiquette which shaped much of social activity. Its social significance is underlined by the recreational use of the Grand Shaft which linked the barracks on the Western Heights with Dover's waterfront. Separate spiral staircases ensured divisions could be marked between promenading couples: the officers and their ladies, the non-commissioned officers and their wives, and the other ranks with their women. Promenades linked the built environment to the seashore. They became a focus for architectural features peculiar to the seaside: seats, lamp posts, railings and shelters ornately cast in iron with motifs of oriental or maritime inspiration. The topography of some seaside towns such as Folkestone and Ventnor allowed the promenade to lead into cliff walks and gardens. Brighton's broad two-level promenade is without rival in Britain.

Transport was essential to new resorts. Regular boats sailed between London and Margate, Kent, with steamer services beginning in 1814 and, by 1835, the resort received over 100,000 visitors each year. Whereas road transport had been previously slow and hazardous, by 1820 Brighton's popularity was fuelled by over 50 coaches a day arriving from London.

From the 1840s the extension of railways to the coast changed the scale and the character of many resorts. Ambitions to serve railway passengers bound for the cross-Atlantic steamer services prompted the construction of the Great Western (Hydro) Hotel in Bristol (1837-9). Rivalling the hotels recently provided at inland spas, such as Cheltenham, it boasted 'Baths, warm, cold, vapour and shower, in the house'. Comparable station hotels in London were soon copied at resort terminals such as Brighton. From the 1860s there was a boom in hotel construction. This included The Clarence, Dover (1863), The Grand, Brighton (1864), and the Grand, Scarborough

(1867). A 'fantastic pile' built at Aberystwyth in 1864, ultimately became the University College of North Wales. The scale and facilities of the hotels enabled the middle class to enjoy the seaside in a style which emulated the wealth and status of earlier visitors.

Increasing free time allowed ever-growing numbers of workers to reach the seaside. In the 1860s Trade Unions successfully campaigned for half days on Saturdays and in 1871 the Bank Holiday was enshrined in legislation. The spreading network of railways enabled mass travel to the coast. Three years after opening, the railway carried 360,000 passengers to Brighton in a six-month period. The railway changed Southend-on-Sea into 'Whitechapel-by-the-Sea'. Scarborough, Southport and Blackpool became the pleasure grounds of Yorkshire and Lancashire factory workers, just as New Brighton attracted Liverpudlians; and Kent and Essex served the capital. The influx of visitors encouraged a change in seaside resorts. Entertainments proliferated, with piers becoming platforms for slot machines and fortune tellers. The existing large hotels were supplemented by smaller and more modest establishments. In the twentieth century these were in turn outnumbered by the boarding houses whose landladies fuelled the jokes of the entertainers playing the pier theatres and music halls.

Resorts diversified to cater for the differing visitors. Bournemouth held out against the railway until the 1870s, thus remaining exclusive to those who travelled by coach to their rented villas. The restorative properties of Bournemouth's pine-scented air had encouraged several sanitoria to open and its clientele was said to be unfavourably biased to the dying and the recuperating. Hove remained select beside the exploding popularity of Brighton as did Southport to Blackpool, and Lytham St Annes to Southport.

Fondness for the coast as a holiday destination ultimately led to an increase in those wishing to live permanently by the sea. As early as 1915 a development company planned a new town to the east of Brighton, originally to be called Anzac-on-Sea, but eventually called Peacehaven. Far from emulating the old resorts it was a housing development on a rigid grid-iron pattern. Development gathered pace from the 1930s as without modern planning controls piecemeal expansion took over; beaches, cliff tops and marsh edges became fringed by bungalows strung out from the resort nodes. In the late 1960s the journalist Kenneth Lindley dubbed this expansion 'bungaloid infection' as he rallied the public against allowing development to destroy the essence of the coast.

Pleasure piers, horizontal and vertical

At the mouths of rivers, or encircling artificial harbours, a pier is usually a solid structure of masonry which acts as a breakwater. The seaside resort is home to the pleasure pier, whose origin is as utilitarian as the harbour piers. Normally constructed of timber or metal piles carrying a walkway or platform, these open-work piers were first built to enable boats to come alongside to unload passengers and baggage. The leisure demands of the seaside resort gave them a secondary function which then evolved with the changing social scene.

Margate's lifeblood was the flow of hoys bringing visitors from the capital and it was essential to replace the pier that was destroyed by a storm in 1808. The new structure was a traditional solid pier built of Whitby stone. In contrast Ryde on the Isle of Wight, where

38 Summer holiday 1999. The Paddle Steamer Preservation Society keeps traditional coastal transport alive with the Waverley. *From Swanage she is steaming east to Weymouth beneath Durlston Head which casual walkers have reached via well-kept gravel paths and stand learning of seabirds, cretacea and geology*

Portsmouth packets had been landing their passengers on the sands, constructed a wooden landing in 1813; this has been described as the first pleasure pier.

Brighton, the destination for London society, was also the departure point for packet boats to Dieppe. Passengers transferred to the beach in rowing boats or less decorously on the broad shoulders of wading fishermen. The engineering skills of Captain Samuel Brown overcame this inconvenience. He had already provided the coaling boats of Newhaven, Lothian, with an innovative chain pier, which borrowed from the principles of suspension bridges, and he opened the new Chain Pier at Brighton in 1822. This answered the needs of the Channel packets and also introduced the idea of a pier having a commercial leisure use. The 350yd (106m) pier stood out into deep water and ended in an 80ft (24m) wide platform for landing passengers. The chains were supported above four clumps of piles, and the iron tower above each clump was designed to contain a small shop or booth which was hired out by the pier's proprietors. The pier excited the curiosity and admiration of promenaders who were charged 2d to walk upon it. In 1824 the Chain Pier received its first steamship, the *Rapid*. A regular service was established to France, steaming three times a week.

It was the importance of attracting London visitors, conveyed by boat, that prompted pier building in Essex and Kent. In 1830 Southend opened a pier 600ft (183m) in length which three years later was extended to 1500ft (457m) to reach across the sands at low water. Across the estuary at Herne Bay, Thomas Telford built a pier 3000ft (914m) long to reach over the tidal sands. However, these early projects did not instantly set off copycat pier building around the country. This came only after the railways had changed a growing number of villages and towns into fast-expanding seaside destinations for the middle, and then working class.

From 1860 to 1900 over 60 piers were built (including rebuilds). This epidemic in pier building has been linked to the changing role of paddle steamers. Initially they provided a reliable alternative to the sailing packets for reaching seaside destinations. Their first appearance was on the Clyde in 1812, where relatively sheltered water enabled steamers to carry the townsfolk of industrialised Lanarkshire to the seaside resorts such as Bute and Helensburgh. Similar services were established within the Bristol Channel, linking the coal-mining areas of South Wales with Avon and Devon. Steamers also plied the Solent from Southampton and Portsmouth to the resorts of the Isle of Wight. When the railway companies extended lines to the resorts, their fares and frequency provided stiff competition for the steamboat operators. The steamers found a new source of revenue in the provision of day trips. The scope for these was increased as each new resort added a pier to its attractions. Weymouth, for example, was home to a locally owned and operated fleet of paddlesteamers.

The demand for new piers enabled engineers to experiment, and they excelled. Eugenius Birch is among the most well known. In just three decades, he contributed to 13 piers including Blackpool North, Brighton West Pier, Aberystwyth, New Brighton, Birnbeck, Bournemouth and Plymouth. Joseph William Wilson designed the pier at Bognor, West Sussex, which was completed in 1864, and that at Teignmouth, Devon, where he used iron screw piles. In Lancashire Sir James Brunlees drew on the experience of laying a railway around the sinking sands of Morecambe Bay, when he constructed Southport's pier, choosing metal piles ending in a disc rather than a point and using water jets to let them down into the sand.

Sir John Betjemin described the elegance of Clevedon Pier, Avon, 'as delicate as a Japanese print in the mist and like an insect in the sunlight'. Its novel appearance is the product of the search for a practical solution to local conditions and for good value materials (**colour plate 9**). There is a 45ft (14m) tidal range, and currents speed under the pier at over five miles an hour. To reduce resistance more slender construction materials were needed and wrought iron rails, originally destined for the South Wales Railway, were put to good use. Work began in 1867 and the result is a lattice of slender girders forming trestles which support eight spans, each of a 100ft (30m).

The piers of the 1860s remained narrow structures with few entertainments. Entrance fees have been cited as a mark of their exclusivity, separating higher class promenaders from the growing numbers of trippers who reached the seaside by railway and steamer. The West Pier at Brighton charged 6d. By the 1880s piers were built and extended to provide space for entertainment. The addition of pavilions provided ballrooms and seating for thousands to enjoy concerts. Engineering skill provided the piers, and architectural flair embellished their buildings with fantastic decoration borrowed indiscriminately from oriental and arabic buildings. Commercialism provided increasingly diverse entertainment; alongside dancing and concerts the Edwardian pier offered slot machines, rifle galleries and sea diving displays.

The great age of pier building ended with the First World War. The uncertain inter-war years were unpropitious for the high level investment and speculation which had supported early projects. The last pier to be built was at Deal, Kent, in 1957. In contrast to its ornate Victorian and Edwardian predecessors elsewhere, it is a functional structure of steel and reinforced concrete. At the seaward end of the 1000ft (305m) promenade is a cafe and bar. The main use, however, is fishing; Deal, which is in easy reach of London, has excellent sea angling and regularly hosts competitions.

Weather, fire and collision, aided by decay, have taken a slow but heavy toll of piers (**39**). In total at least 90 pleasure piers were built, but by the mid-1980s fewer than 50 resorts had surviving piers. The Isle of Wight, for example, was noted for the number of piers built in the 1860s to 90s. Nine day trip and resort destinations had piers, of which only Totland, Yarmouth, Ryde and Sandown now survive. The most recent pier casualty was at Bognor in an October storm 1999.

The Eiffel Tower inspired the construction of towers as seaside attractions. Like the pier these combined the escapism of imaginative architecture, the promise of a panorama and novelty entertainment. Blackpool's famous tower was built in 1894. Three years later New Brighton, Cheshire, opened a taller rival. The latter could not be adequately maintained during the First World War and was subsequently demolished. Today's visitors are reminded of the resort's heyday by the inclusion of the sites of both the pier and the tower amidst the modern facilities and attractions on street-mounted tourist maps.

Novelty transport

The railway terminus with families laden for a week's holiday created a need for local transport. Pony traps, goat carts and boys with hand barrows proliferated to serve the paying customer. As the emphasis on pleasure grew, so imaginative engineering projects made a crossover between utilitarian transport and entertainment. Among these were the cliff railways, of which some 25 were built on the coast between the 1870s and the 1930s. The majority were operational in 1964; passengers are still carried at Saltburn-by-the-Sea, Folkestone, Hastings, Bournemouth and Aberystwyth.

Funicular railways and overhead cable cars are usually associated with mountain ski resorts. However engineers at the British seaside were ahead of their continental colleagues. Employing technology from the early industrial railways they used cable haulage to pull passenger cars up from the seashore. Steep gradients were typical, ranging from 1:1.23 at Southend to 1:2 at Aberystwyth; the 1:2.8 at Torquay was positively gentle. The need for motive power was reduced by using the downward car, sometimes with water ballast, as a counter-balance. This was emptied at the lower station and either pumped to a reservoir at the upper or discharged, as at Lynmouth, into the sea. The cars were either mounted on rails or suspended from overhead cables. Between 12 and 40 passengers were accommodated in each car. Variations in car construction included a horizontal-floor mounted on a triangular underframe, or a stepped floor (**40**).

Cliff railways were usually proposed where speculators could anticipate sufficient passengers to bring a return on their capital investment, and so they were a feature of the

39 Remains of Swanage Pier. This decayed hardwood pile demonstrates the difficulties to be faced in maintaining nineteenth century piers. The display supported fundraising for a new pier

busy, cliff-backed resorts. The first was opened in 1876, on the initiative of Mr Hunt of the Prince of Wales Hotel in Scarborough. His South Cliff Lift gave the hotel's clientele easy access to the promenade below. A second line, the Central Tramway, was constructed in 1880. Four years later, Saltburn-by-the-Sea opened a line rising 207ft (63m) from the pier. The following year Folkestone opened a double-track cliff railway at the Leas, which in 1890 was uniquely expanded to provide four lines. The railway built to link Lynmouth with Lynton was cut through solid rock and opened in 1890 at a length of 900ft (274m).

The integration of the cliff railway with traditional seaside pursuits can be appreciated at Aberystwyth. From the end of the promenade the 798ft (243m) line hauls passengers 500ft (152m) to the top of Constitution Hill. It is crossed by numerous bridges carrying the walkways by which promenaders once roamed through gardens to the summit. Here stands the restored camera obscura still providing uninterrupted views of Cardigan Bay. On the opening Sunday in 1895 the railway carried 520 passengers at fares of 8d to 1s. A further 810 travelled for sixpence on the Monday.

Construction continued in the twentieth century with cliff railways at Hastings (1903), Bournemouth (1908), Broadstairs (1910), Margate (1912), Southend (1912) and Torquay (1926). The last to be built was at Fisherman's Walk, Bournemouth in 1935. This

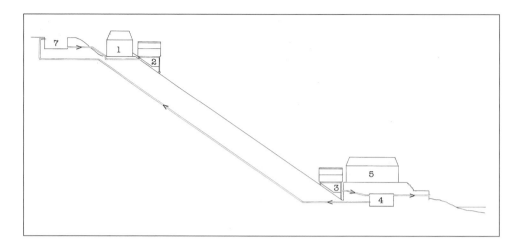

40 *Cliff railways use a water-balance system as an alternative or supplement to engines*
1 *The wheel house is the operation centre. Here a brake can be applied to the central pulley wheel, around which pass the cables that link the two cars. This controls the speed of descent/ascent*
2 *Water is let into the tank beneath the upper car until it is heavier than the lower car. The imbalance sets the upper car in motion, hauling the lower car to the summit as it decends*
3 *On reaching the bottom water is let out of the car*
4 *The water is either held in a storage tank or allowed to flow as waste into the sea*
5 *Pumps in the lower station return water to the summit*
6 *A river, or a reservoir refilled by the pumps, supplies water for the upper car*

was the town's third, a number equalled by Folkestone, while Scarborough had four.

At Brighton a ride above the waves was made possible by the Volks Railway built in 1883. Its tracks were below low water, and the passenger car was supported on stilts while electric power came from overhead lines. Some remains of the tracks can sometimes still be seen at low tide. Its route is mirrored by the miniature railway that now runs from the pier to the Marina. While miniature railways, such as on Hastings Beach, are ridden for entertainment, today's holidaymakers require road-based transport within resorts. So-called road-trains provide this while, in their decoration, they draw on the imagery of steam railways as the fun-transport of the seaside.

In the late 1950s Butlins added a new attraction to their Holiday Camp at Ayr. A 520yd (158m) long chair lift carried diners up a 123ft (38m) rise to the restaurant. Longer lifts were installed at the holiday camps in Pwllheli, Filey and Skegness to carry people down to the sea front. The Pleasure Beach at Blackpool enjoyed the fares of a possible 800 passengers an hour on its 1166ft (355m) long chair lift installed in 1961. The chair lift descending to the beach at Alum Bay, Isle of Wight added a theme-park style ride to the natural attractions of the cliffs coloured sands.

Activity explosion

The last three decades have seen massive expansion in the number of people participating in watersports for leisure, with individual sports being the major growth areas. Windsurfing, for instance, was introduced to Britain in 1974 and within 15 years had an estimated half million casual participants. Team sports have not disappeared and Dragon Boats are a notable newcomer with crews of 20 paddlers, a drummer and a steersman racing in sheltered coastal waters and reused docks. The influx of people at weekends and holidays has become large enough to threaten the coastline. The passage of cars and people can, for example, easily erode areas of sand dunes or thin cliff-top soils.

Management initiatives which aim for sustainable leisure use of the coast have often enabled elements of the coastal heritage to be consolidated and interpreted for the public. The purchase of coastal land by the National Trust, the creation of Heritage Coasts, country parks and long distance coast paths have all contributed to this work.

At the mouth of Southampton Water the Calshot Activity Centre and Lepe Country Park are examples. The coastal country park has large car parks with a cafe and easy beach access. This provides a focal point for windsurfers, walkers, and the carbound. New sea defences have protected a construction site for caissons, destined to form a harbour during the Normandy landings, while the original service roads provide easy walking for visitors. The park runs north towards Calshot Spit which has a many faceted history. Its tip is still capped by one of Henry VIII's castles (33), a lifeboat station and coastguard watch tower. The creation of an Activity Centre has given new use to the huge hangars of a Royal Naval Flying Boat Base which opened in 1913. These now house dinghies, canoes, windsurfing boards, a velodrome and climbing walls, while a heritage trail can introduce the visitor to the original layout and work of the site.

8 Havens and markets: creating ports and harbours

> The challenge to secure and possibly extend the seaborne trade depended on
> the capacity of the townspeople and their immediate neighbours to provide
> safe access and adequate docking facilities... Adams, 1993. In Jackson (ed) *The
> Port of Montrose*

The diverse and intensive use of the coast described in the preceding chapters has in many
instances only been possible with the aid of boats and ships. Ports and harbours ensured
their safekeeping and efficient work. Despite the ravages of the sea innumerable examples
survive, often centuries after a specialist activity, such as pilchard fishing or alum
production, has ceased. The construction of a port or harbour provides a tool to facilitate
the five uses of the coast and sea: extraction of resources, waste disposal, transport, defence
and leisure.

Ports and harbours differ immensely in scale, complexity, purpose and antiquity.
Nineteenth-century Liverpool, for example, boasted seven miles (11km) of purpose-built
docks ranged along the riverfront. Elsewhere, however, harbours comprised only a narrow
cliff-hemmed river as at Staithes, Yorkshire, or a cove such as Polperro, Cornwall, while
on the open coast harbours could only be provided by manmade breakwaters.

The defining characteristic of a port is that it provides facilities for ships to load and
unload cargo or passengers while a harbour is no more than a shelter for ships. This might
be a natural feature such as the bay at Swanage, Dorset, the drowned ria of Plymouth
Sound, Devon, or a river like the Aeron at Aberaeron, Dyfed. Such natural shelters may
be enhanced, perhaps by a lone breakwater such as the Cobb at Lyme Regis, Dorset, or by
complex engineering schemes. A harbour then is only one facility of a port, enabling ships
to lie safely at anchor or aground. To handle cargo a port will add facilities such as
equipment for lifting and moving, storage, and transport to carry goods to markets inland
or along the coast. Surveying and dredging, setting navigation markers and providing
pilots are also port services which contribute to the safety of visiting ships.

It is difficult to pigeonhole the huge variety of ports into groups. A list ranking ports
by size, for example, will change with the method of measuring: volume of cargo handled,
value of cargo handled or number of ship movements. Some ports and harbours have
been built to facilitate individual coastal uses: ferry ports to transport people, naval bases
for defence, and marinas for leisure. However one port often serves many uses, in the way
that Portsmouth Harbour holds a ferry port, naval base and marinas. Attempts at
geographic classifications include river ports such as Sunderland, tidal estuary ports like

1 'Submerged Forest', Marros Sands, Dyfed. Low tide reveals an extensive and thick layer of decayed vegetation. Twigs and small branches can be seen in its surface. With sand washed from the beach, the sea erodes the grey/blue clay beneath, undermining the peat so that large chunks break away

2 Seabed peat and forest
Top: Investigating peat lenses in a seabed cliff beneath the Solent. (Garry Momber)
Bottom: A lobster has burrowed into peat, beneath an exposed tree trunk. The upcast from such bur-
rows has included flints worked by humans. (Garry Momber)

3 Baited traps laid on the seabed to catch crab or lobster have regionally specific names. Fishermen are adept at using readily available materials; and substitutes have been found for the traditional with-ies, wood and netting of nat-ural fibres

a) Whitby. The trap has a base of sawn timbers. Plastic hoops support hazel sticks which carry the netting

b) Craster. Scrap iron is a mod-ern substitute for the tradi-tional stone weight used here. From a decayed trap made entirely from natural materi-als the stone might be the only component to survive. The wear from the binding yarn would betray its use, and marine growth show it had been in the sea, but how con-fident would any archaeologist be to state it was part of a baited trap?

c) Dunbar. Plastic drums imagi-natively recycled as baited traps. The remains of old traps are in the background

4   Brick-Lined Sewer, Brighton. In 1865 work began to lay 44 miles of sewer ranging from 12"
diameter glazed drain pipes to circular tunnels 8 ft (2.4m) high. Amidst controversy an intercept-
ing sewer was completed in 1874 to carry waste to discharge into the sea at Portobello, beyond the
borough boundary. Today visitors can be guided through sections of the Victorian sewer (Southern
Water)

*5 The woolhouse, Southampton, Hampshire is now a maritiem museum. It is typical warehousing for a medieval customs port. The tiled roof is upported on timber beams and rafters; compare this with nineteenth-century bonded warehouses (**colour plate 12**)*

6&7 *Limekilns betray the transport by sea of limestone for making lime and/or coal for fuel*

a) In Loch Eriboll, Highland, a causewayed island has a bank of four kilns surrounded by quarries

b) The top of the kiln is a round opening through which the charge of limestone and coal are loaded. The interior is lined with brick

c) The arched entrance to the draw hole is large enough for a cart to load lime undercover

d) At Solva, Dyfed, one of six small round kilns standing against the cliff of the natural harbour. In contrast to (c) the entrance to the draw hole is only large enough for a person

e) At an isolated settlement on the Highland coast are the grassed over remains of a collapsed beach-side limekiln

8   *Naturally defensive sites have attracted coastal settlement since prehistory. Eilean Donan Castle,*
    Highland (top) was built in 1220 on a small island at confluence of Loch Duich and Loch Alsh
    and is now reached via a bridge. The castle would have been defensible against attack from the
    shore or boats carrying archers. It was not however a coast defence in the modern sense and was
    destroyed by a naval bombardment in 1719. The spectacular location of Dunnottar Castle,
    Grampian (bottom), built between the fourteenth and sixteenth centuries, on a 160ft high crag
    compares with the defensive cliff sites of prehistory

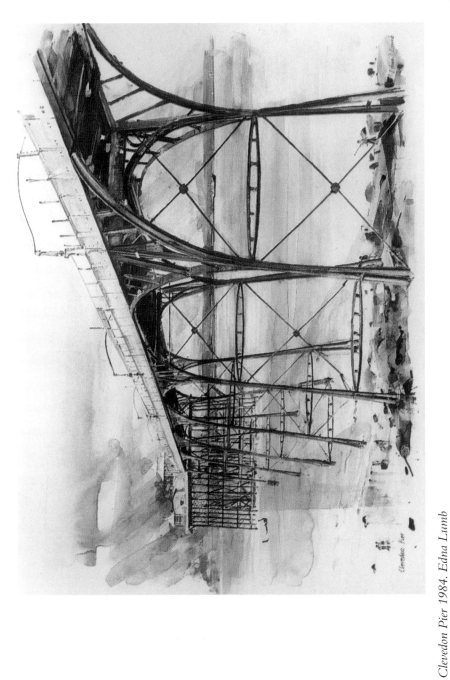

9 *Clevedon Pier 1984. Edna Lumb*
Built in 1867 the unique construction is a result of combating severe tidal conditions and using competitively priced materials. Commissioned to support the repair fund and here reproduced courtesy of the Edna Lumb Artistic Trust. Flat 2, 14 The Paragon, Blackheath, London, SE3 0PA (Available as Limited Edition Print)

10 *Portsoy Harbour, Highland was prosperous enough to construct a harbour in 1692, around which the houses and warehouses are still huddled for protection from the elements*

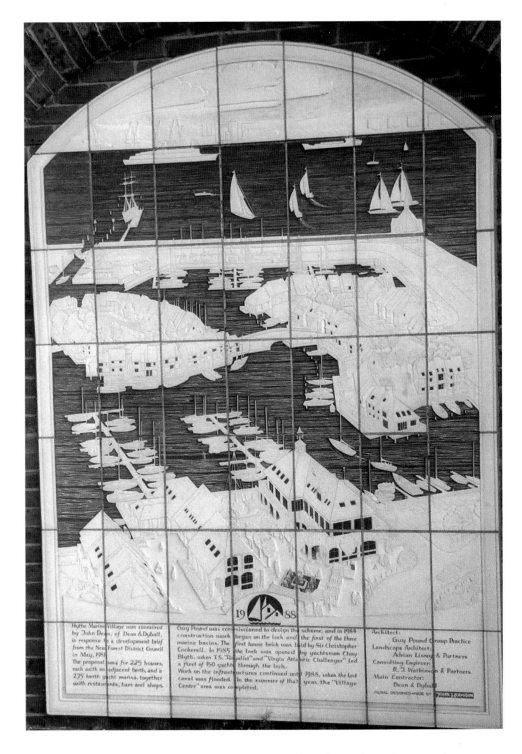

11 *Hythe Marina, Hampshire. The commemorative wall tessellation shows the narrow houses crowded onto the short stretches of waterfront*

12 *Albert Dock, Liverpool (1845). Square-shaped docks provided space for many small ships to lie safely afloat, with those at the quaysides unloading directly into warehouses. The narrowness of entrance locks, however, limited their value as the size of iron ships increased. Slender internal columns (cross section) can be seen rising from the foundations to support five floors. The use of stone, brick and iron throughout minimised fire risk*

13 *Bucklers Hard, Hampshire. The huge timbers of the slipway have been excavated at this eighteenth-century shipbuilding village. The main street flanked by brick-built workers houses is in
the background. (Garry Momber)*

14 *Hartlepool Renaissance. The shipbuilding yards of Hartlepool which were opened in the nine-teenth century were demolished and their dry docks filled in for redevelopment. Creation of a her-itage attraction saw one dock re-excavated (Top). The steel frame buildings erected alongside were then dressed with historical facades and the dock flooded to re-create an eighteenth-century water-front (Bottom)*

15 *right: Girdleness Lighthouse, Aberdeen, was built 1833 by Robert Stevenson and fits the popular image of a lighthouse as a slender tower. Below: at St Abbs, David & Thomas Stevenson's choice of a squat building shows that a tower atop the high cliffs would only have disappeared into low cloud or fog. In poor visibility foghorns supplemented the light. The horn stands on the cliff edge and the riveted compressed air tanks are behind the lighthouse. An American-made foghorn was installed at St Abbs (1862) sometime before 1880*

16 Dramatic change brings to the fore the challenge of contemporary collecting and preservation. Will the dismembered pieces of 1990s fishing boats at some later date be valued in the way that care is devoted to the fragile timbers of the frigate Unicorn (1824) lying afloat in the far left corner of this Dundee dock?

Glasgow on the Clyde, and artificial harbours such as Seaham on the Durham coast. While these reveal little about the activities served by the port, each geographic type has particular operating problems in common. Major dredging, for example, has been essential to the success of tidal estuary ports.

The development and maintenance of complex port facilities requires capital and organisation of local shipping interests. In surveying the archaeology of ports economic historian Gordon Jackson grouped them according to the developments which they had undertaken. This approach can highlight both uses of the coast as stimulants to the growth of individual ports and the influence of geographic characteristics in either their success or failure.

Boats and small ships can easily handle cargo between tides while lying aground in the mud of a river or on a gently shelving beach. Wheelbarrows could traverse a plank between riverbank and deck while ropes and pulleys, hoisted in the rigging, provided effective lifting gear. Carts carrying cargo from ships on the shore were a common sight in the nineteenth century and at a few ports, such as Hastings in East Sussex, fishing fleets can still be seen on the beach. Improvements only become necessary when natural facilities prove inadequate for the number of visiting ships. Prospering river ports, sheltered from both storms and pirates, attracted most vessels but soon needed to improve their banks since erosion caused by ships' wake left mud foreshores on which unloading was difficult (**41**).

41 Harbour Works (1992). A double-ended boat has been used to reform a breakwater destroyed by the sea. In the distance are broken parts of boats that the sea has already eroded from the new structure. In the quieter waters of rivers, banks were effectively consolidated by burying old boats

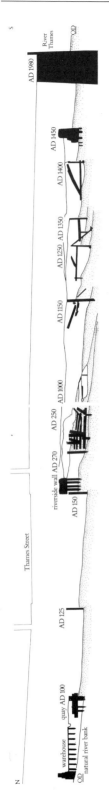

42 London's Waterfront has slowly advanced with the construction of each new river revetment; earlier structures becoming sealed beneath the built up ground level. This simplified 100m north-south section shows the sequence with approximate dates. (Courtesy Gustav Milne.)

Most of port facilities that are visible today were constructed to cope with successive expansions in trade from the sixteenth century (**colour plate 10**). Port facilities are not, however, exclusive to the post-medieval period. Excavation in London, for example, has revealed the development of the Roman port. The earliest improvement was made in the mid-first century and consisted of a gravel embankment reinforced by wooden piles and faced with a revetment of posts and planks to contain the river. By the end of the century the waterfront stood 15m (49ft) forward and comprised a framework of horizontal timber baulks behind which the ground was built up to 2m (6ft 6in) above flood level. To the east a similar waterfront, some 75m (245ft) long, had replaced a landing stage of open timber work which would have required gangplanks to transfer people and goods to the shore. No fewer than five open-fronted storage buildings, *horrea*, lined the quayside. Following a fire in the second century the waterfront was reconstructed a further 25m (82ft) forward with new 'warehousing'. Now at a distance from the quay, the original *horrea* appear to have become used as shops. By the time the final Roman waterfront was built in the third century some 50m (164ft) of land had been claimed from the river foreshore (**42**).

The Roman waterfronts are of massive construction using timbers up to 66 x 40cm in cross section (2ft 2in x 1ft 4in). In comparison with some 20 examples of medieval waterfronts found in London which were effectively constructed from much lesser scantlings, the Roman use of timber has been described as profligate and their engineering attributed to the Imperial army. Alternatives to timber revetments were described in the medieval period. In 1344, on the narrow creek at Arbroath, the Abbot's master of works supervised local inhabitants in filling coffers with stones. The ferrymen of Hythe, Hampshire, were obliged to bring boatloads of stone to protect the walls of Southampton (**32**) against erosion by either the tide or ships' wash. Medieval river ports also concerned themselves with preventing silting. Barges at Sandwich in Kent, for instance, were expected to periodically travel down

43 *The Butterfly Boat, Rye, Sussex. This twentieth-century variation on rake-towing barges of medieval Sandwich travelled downstream with its 'wings' spread to stir up the sediments so they would be flushed by the outgoing tide. (Courtesy Clifford Bloomfield)*

the River Stour towing a rake over the stern to stir up the sediment (**43**).

River ports, whose modest waterfronts had served medieval ships, faced ruin as more capacious ports nearer to the sea captured the rapidly expanding trades. They fought back with improvements to overcome winding and silted river channels. In the 1560s Exeter cut a channel to make navigation possible up river from Topsham, Devon. Extended in the 1670s, this served throughout the eighteenth century. Similar projects elsewhere failed to revive ailing ports including Chester, which made a cut on the heavily silted Dee in the 1730s, Grimsby in Yorkshire, and Colchester in Essex. As late as 1808 Stockton straightened and deepened the River Tees in Cleveland, but despite doubling the tonnage visiting the port it could not compete with down-river Middlesborough.

The bulk of foreign trade was increasingly focused on a relatively small number of ports whose position on major rivers linked them to extensive hinterlands. These ports redistributed foreign goods coastwise and by inland navigation, and drew to them commodities not only for export, but foodstuffs, fuels and building materials to supply their own rapidly expanding populations. Their demands made the creation of port facilities viable elsewhere, most notably by building protective piers on coasts without natural havens.

Most numerous among these pier ports are the small eighteenth- and nineteenth-century fishing harbours of Cornwall. Similar harbours in Scotland (**44**) were built so fishing could provide a new livelihood for families forcibly relocated to the coast by landowners. Once the shoals had moved or been fished out, however, there was no other commodity to export, and the surrounding communities were too small to generate trade by their own demand for goods. Minerals were the other key export of pier ports. St Ives, Cornwall, was built to export tin and its imports comprised mainly machinery and

44 Latheronwheel, Highland. The harbour is typical of small pier ports where breakwaters provide protection within a natural cove but there are no additional facilities for lifting, storing or transporting cargoes. The road leads through a winding valley to the village

supplies for mining communities. Like the fishing ports, small harbours built to export from cliff quarries, such as Port Mulgrave which shipped iron ore, had no hinterland and no alternative trade.

The profits promised by coal-mining spawned one of the most unusual pier ports, Seaham Harbour. County Durham's coal was carried by rail to the River Wear where keels transferred it to ships at Sunderland. Resenting the high costs, the Marquis of Londonderry began building a new harbour on Durham's rocky coast in 1828. Coal was first shipped in 1831 but the harbour was only completed in 1845 as, in place of simple piers, it comprised an outer and inner dock, with coal fed by gravity from the cliff above. Unlike other pier ports, the scale and sophistication of Seaham, with rail and later road links to inland towns, provided a port which was viable even when coal shipments declined.

The financial loss caused by shipwrecks also prompted expenditure on pier ports. The hundreds-strong collier fleets beating down the east coast had few places of natural safety between the Tees and the Wash. As early as 1697 Bridlington, Yorkshire, was granted duties from coal to provide piers to shelter colliers. Similarly funded, Scarborough improved and extended its piers throughout the eighteenth century. Many ships approaching London awaited fair weather in the Downs, off Kent, before entering the Thames. The anchorage afforded no shelter and so, in 1749, Ramsgate was proposed as a harbour of refuge. Storm damage made this early work slow and costly since there was little understanding of the techniques and materials necessary for piers in exposed

45 *The grab-dredger,* Ramsgate *is ideal for working close to piers. The piers at Ramsgate were built to form a harbour of refuge; it has since prospered as a cross-Channel ferry terminal. In the background are the chalk cliffs of the natural shoreline*

locations. Like other pier ports where there is no river, the still water within the harbour rapidly deposited silt (**45**). This was overcome by constructing an inner basin as a reservoir to flush the outer harbour. An early flushing or sluicing basin also survives at Tenby, Dyfed.

While many places were improved by piers and were busy with coastal shipping the great volume of eighteenth-century trade centered on the major commercial ports. Since these were also river ports their main problem was congestion. Small ships crowded their often tidal quays while cargoes were commonly carried by lighters to larger vessels afloat in the channel or river mouth. Voyages had to coincide with good weather months, and ships laid up for winter added to the crowding. Between 1697 and 1700 an entrepreneurial landowner provided a laying-up facility by creating the 10-acre Howland Great Wet Dock at Rotherhithe on the Thames. Liverpool developed the idea further by opening a cargo-handling dock. This was safer and more efficient than the river shore at the relatively unsheltered mouth of the Mersey. However, vessels awaiting tides and weather overcrowded the dock and once conditions were fair it was impossible for all to exit at once. The Corporation responded by enlarging the entrance to form a tidal basin where vessels might safely lie, and by building a second dock.

Elsewhere the need for both capital and consensus among merchant interests limited dock building. In the 1770s Hull constructed Britain's first large commercial dock, some 9 acres. Whereas Liverpool Corporation continued adding small docks as trade grew, the private company which financed Hull's dock obstructed further building and the port only opened a second in 1809. Bristol took over half a century to reach agreement in 1803 over a dock which, by diverting the Avon, incorporated the existing quaysides thus creating a Floating Harbour.

By the 1790s the Port of London was desperately overcrowded both afloat and ashore, especially as its legal quays were too short to handle the huge volume of goods subject to customs dues. The need to combat custom-dodging and theft contributed to companies being authorised to build docks for handling trade from specific regions and to receive dues from the ships carrying them. The West India Docks opened in 1802, comprising 30 acres for imports and 24 acres for exports, and the London Dock, for European trades, in 1803. Unlike docks in Hull and Liverpool these were secured behind high perimeter walls and had immense warehouses. Enclosed docks were built for other trades until trade monopolies came under attack and St Katharine's Dock Company was formed in 1832 by advocates of free trade. The surviving dock represents the last phase of the enclosed system with cargo handling directly between ship and warehouses which stand flush with the quayside supported on iron columns to allow quay space beneath. The same principle can be seen in the bonded warehouses of Albert Dock, Liverpool (1845), where iron and brick were used throughout to reduce fire risk (**colour plate 12**).

Docks and quayside warehouses were not suited to handling bulky cargoes such as timber and minerals. In addition those located in the crowded mercantile areas of the major ports had little chance of adapting to the changing face of shipping and land transport. Outside there was no room to route railways, which were replacing canals as the arteries of the hinterlands, while inside their locks were too small and their quays too confined to admit steamers whose iron hulls were rapidly increasing in size. Opened in 1855, London's 100-acre Victoria Dock embraced these changes with an 80ft wide lock and 1/2 mile long quays, piers giving extra berthing for the area of water, the port's first hydraulic cranes, and transit sheds enabling cargo to be sorted and moved from ships to the railway which encircled the dock.

Interaction with railways was not new. For centuries they had carried coal to the North East's ports with horse-drawn and then cable-hauled wagons. Locomotives had been introduced on the Stockton & Darlington Railway in 1825 and within a year the company was operating coal staithes at Stockton. Railway companies began initiating dock building, often choosing new locations to which goods could be carried overland by rail thus circumventing existing port facilities. Fierce competition multiplied their projects which contributed to the development of coaling ports in the North West, notably Mary Port, Workington and Whitehaven, and in South Wales especially at Newport, Cardiff, Barry, Penarth, Port Talbot, Swansea and Llanelli.

Steam transport also brought competition among packet ports, handling passengers and mail. The short sea crossing had made Dover the traditional link with the continent, even receiving help from Henry VIII to build an early pier. In 1844 a railway from London confirmed Dover's importance but rival rail companies developed the neighbouring harbours of Folkestone and Newhaven. As peace prevailed and steamships became more reliable, short sea-crossings were less paramount. Falmouth lost favour as a packet port after 1840 when the London and Southampton railway revived the latter's decayed port. Then the construction of a dock, in 1842, attracted to Southampton the prestigious Peninsular & Orient Steam Navigation Company, Royal Mail Steam Packet Company and

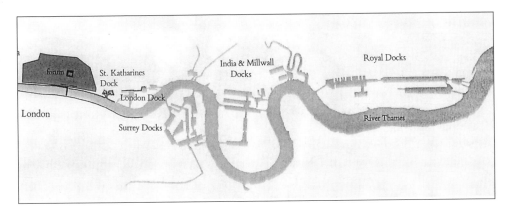

46 London's Roman harbour (south of the forum), formed the port facilities of a small province within the Empire, they are dwarfed by the docks built to serve the nineteenth-century capital of the British Empire. (Courtesy Gustav Milne)

the Union Steamship Company, which served the outstations of Britain's Empire.

The volume of trade vastly expanded in the late nineteenth century. Foreign and coastal shipping increased from some 37 million tons in 1870/4 to 94 millions in 1910/13. Much comprised bulk cargoes, such as coal, grain and cotton, with low freight rates. Quick turn arounds were essential to both shipowners and crowded ports, and emphasis fell on providing lengthy open quays, transit sheds no more than two storeys high, and machinery for cargo handling. While Southampton could provide river quays, which later received the greatest liners, adjacent to deep water channels, others enlarged and built new docks with massive locks to take the largest ships afloat. For example, the Royal Edward Dock, Avonmouth (1908), was 30 acres and 36ft (11m) deep with a lock 875 x 100ft (267 x 30m).

The alternative to docks was artificially deepened river berths. River ports had striven to combat shoals by improving natural scouring. Glasgow expended huge sums and great hope on building training walls to narrow the Clyde so as to increase the force of the outflowing river. Later engineers reversed this so that the greater volume of water entering on the flood would increase the scour on the ebb tide. Eventually the riverbed was remodelled by steam dredging. The first steam dredger was seen in 1797 at Sunderland. By 1840 the Clyde had five at work while the Tyne Improvement Commission, formed only in 1851, employed six dredgers by the mid 1860s, removing up to 5 million tons per annum. Deepening the Tyne to 20ft (6m) as far as Newcastle enabled colliers to use riverside staithes while the depth in the Clyde was increased from 19ft in 1858 to 30ft in 1902 (5.8m to 9.1m) and later maintained so that the largest liners built by Browns could safely leave the river.

Imported oil was the new bulk trade but tankers with flammable cargoes requiring shoreside storage were ill-suited to existing docks, although some large coaling docks were converted at Swansea and Grangemouth in the 1920s. Elsewhere tankers were soon accommodated at piers from which the oil was piped ashore to 'tank farms'. These piers had the advantage of standing into deep water and so accommodating the slow increase in the size of tankers.

The twentieth century brought further major changes in cargo handling. Traditionally goods had been transported in units which could be easily moved by hand, and this method of carriage changed little through the centuries. The principal survivors of Roman cargoes, for example, are ceramic containers, amphoras, used to carry goods such as wine, oil and olives. While the wool bales exported from medieval England are unlikely to have survived, seventeenth-century shipwrecks have shown that ceramic containers remained in use for commodities as diverse as fruit and mercury. Barrels are commonly found on shipwrecks since they were used through to the modern period, not only for liquids but for packing objects including coins and clay pipes.

A man-powered treadmill crane at Harwich is an unusual example of lifting equipment in use by the eighteenth century. Hydraulic power was successfully applied to cranes by Armstrong's of Newcastle in 1846. Although water towers, pipes and cranes (**50**) became a common feature of docks the unit of general cargo remained small, as once on the quayside it was sorted and moved manually. It was not until the 1950s that forklift trucks were used in docks to lift pallets on which goods were secured by metal straps. These straps were also effective in bundling hitherto unmanageable timber into units which could be lifted mechanically. Increasing motorised road transport and the effectiveness of vehicle landing craft in the Second World War showed the way to develop ships for carrying roll-on/roll-off cargoes. Modern cargo handling was embraced when, in 1956, the Port of London initiated the essential collaboration which enabled containers to be introduced for carrying general cargo. By forming a standard unit for transfer from ship to road or rail, these eliminated manual handling and reduced turn around time from weeks to days. While the existing major ports converted or extended their accommodation for container ships, an entirely new container-handling facility was created at Felixstowe, which was well-placed for European trade and the hinterland of both London and the Midlands.

Witnessing older port facilities becoming redundant and facing re-use, in 1983, Gordon Jackson commented that 'it seems unlikely that outside the currently working docks little will remain to show how ports looked before *c.*1960'. In the 1990s, however, it remains possible to see some older port facilities by visiting redevelopments which have preserved, albeit in a sanitised form, elements of docks and warehouses. Prime examples include St Katharine's Dock next to the Tower of London, Albert Dock in Liverpool (**colour plate 12**), and Gloucester Docks home of the National Waterways Museum (**49**).

9 Making and breaking: boat and shipbuilding

> I believe the boat to have been the most important invention that man has ever made. You can eat raw food, you can walk thousands of miles without a cart, but you cannot populate the globe without a boat. Lethbridge, 1952. *Boats and Boatmen*

Boatbuilders provided the essential tool which enabled humankind to use the resources of the coast from the sea. As seagoing craft became larger and more complex shipbuilding employed specialist workers, including sawyers, shipwrights, caulkers and riggers, and used the products of many tradesmen such as pumpmakers, ropemakers, blockmakers, sailmakers and blacksmiths and iron founders. Permanent shipyards only became necessary as vessels grew larger and new technology such as the construction of iron hulls and fitting of engines required expenditure on machinery. Many nineteenth-century shipyards have been cleared as part of waterfront development while the ephemeral remains of earlier shipbuilding sites have long since been lost.

For the centuries before extensive written records exist the principle evidence for boatbuilding comes from surviving craft. The information which they yield depends on the way in which they have been preserved and the care employed in recording them. The timbers of wrecked ships, for example, may survive in soft seabed sediments but their iron fastenings such as nails or bolts have often corroded away. In contrast the Saxon boats placed in burials on the sandy soil of the Suffolk coast have lost their timbers but the iron which fastened the planking survives.

The timbers of surviving craft have gone from 'tree to sea'. They betray the boatbuilder's art. Their unworn surfaces bear the marks of axes, adzes, chisels and saws. Each tool mark is individual because it shows any defect in the cutting edge and is as characteristic as a signature. The sculpting of individual components show how the builder formed the complex shape of the craft and this reveals his understanding of how the boat or ship would perform under oars or sail. The timbers also show the species, age and shape of tree from which they were cut. So boats can provide special clues to the sources of wood used by coastal dwellers and to their control of woodland. Much can also be gleaned about levels of community organisation by studying the logistical challenge and time required to select and fell trees, shape the timbers and transport either these or the finished craft, to the sea. Later ships like the *Mary Rose* were built from hundreds of trees and she is a unique resource for studying Tudor woodland management. Examination of her timbers has been coupled with research into the accounts of nearby

47 Modern skin boat. The remains of such craft are missing from Britain's archaeological record, but how easy would it be to recognise animal hide, woven withy and a forked stick as the components of a boat?

local estates, such as those of the Oglander family at Nunwell on the Isle of Wight, which supplied trees for shipbuilding.

Knowledge of early boatbuilding is biased by surviving craft. The most common British discoveries from prehistory are either logboats or plankboats of oak. Yet anthropological studies and the earliest written records show how probable it is that other materials were being used. Boats made from animal skins stretched over light frameworks of wood (**47**), or even antler, are very serviceable on rivers, while Irish curraghs show their capabilities as seagoing vessels. Decayed or disassembled, the components of such vessels may be difficult to recognise as boat parts. This can also be true of plank boats as Valerie Fenwick wryly demonstrated by reinterpreting a museum object labelled as 'wooden lid with a handle' as a 'reused plank with integral cleat' from a Bronze Age-type boat.

With only hand tools and manpower the construction of boats and even early ships need leave no trace beyond a layer of wood chippings and perhaps some discarded timbers. The discovery of no fewer than five Bronze Age boat fragments on the Humber foreshore at North Ferriby invites the idea that this was a place where boats were used and repaired, if not built. Old vessels were certainly a feature of later shipbuilding sites. For example, the detailed accounts for the construction of the *Grace Dieu* between 1416 and 1418 record at least two ships purchased so that they could be broken for timber. Ship breaking became a specialist activity of later shipyards. Unfortunately, as far as archaeological evidence is

48 HMS Victory's *fore topsail. Momentarily transported from the hubbub of Portsmouth's Festival of the Sea, visitors quietly stared in wonder at the tattered canvas and actually read the information boards below. The sail is a rare survivor from the dozens carried by each of the hundreds of naval sailing ships. The weight of canvas has been supported on netting so it could once again be bent to a yard suspended in the modern dockyard shed*

concerned, it is self-destroying, except where re-used components can be found. River revetments are often built from old ships' timbers but the most remarkable discovery was made at Chatham Historic Dockyard in 1995. Beneath the floor of a wheelwright's shop lay 169 timbers, the earliest dated by dendrochronology to *c*.1690, which came possibly from a single eighteenth-century warship. They were so fresh as to still carry tool marks and paint plus the marks and initials of individual carpenters.

Documentary references to shipbuilding show that one-off vessels could be built on sheltered beaches or riverbanks. The construction site needed only a flat or gently shelving area of firm ground on which to lay the keel, supported on horizontal timbers (**32**). A bank or fence might surround the area to deter thieving of precious timber. Scaffolds for work as the hull grew higher, and timber shear-legs for lifting heavy beams or stepping masts were all temporary. Where numbers of ships were built in the same place some facilities might become more permanent. Pits were used by sawyers cutting large timbers with two-man saws; ponds were dug to season timbers; and ropes were made by twisting hemp yarn along the lengths of narrow ropewalks. Such features appear on early estate plans, tithe maps and first edition Ordnance Survey maps or have been preserved in field or street names and can sometimes be located by archaeological surveys.

In 1689 a major programme of naval shipbuilding began. Since the naval dockyards could not meet the urgent deadlines, contracts were given to private builders close by. New warships were built on the rivers and creeks around the Solent, including the Beaulieu River where Bucklers Hard became a permanent shipbuilding site throughout the eighteenth century. The village has long been a visitor attraction with a small museum explaining the construction of warships and a broad 'street' leading between two rows of workers' houses to the peaceful river side where grassy depressions were all that could be seen of the shipbuilding. In the summers since 1993 visitors watched a new spectacle as students and volunteers excavated the riverbank. Working in mud at low water and diving at highwater the team revealed the substantial structure of a slipway which unexpectedly survived beneath the grass. It was built of huge horizontal timbers, set down in layers, designed to carry the weight of wooden ships perhaps 150ft (45.7m) in length (**colour plate 13**).

The Naval Dockyards themselves represent permanent shipbuilding and repairing facilities. At both Portsmouth and Chatham it is possible to see the complex of buildings which contributed to construction, albeit altered and with new uses. The fundamental process of wooden ship construction saw few changes between the sixteenth and nineteenth centuries. A massive, straight timber was laid as the keel or backbone of the ship. For longer vessels this would be formed of two timbers joined, or scarfed, together. The stem and sternpost were then set up on the keel. The shape of the ship was usually taken from a model, and the outline of each frame was drawn onto the floor of a building called a moulding loft. From this template moulds were cut, against which the timbers were shaped and then joined together and set on the keel to form the skeleton of the ship's sides. Immense strength was achieved by selecting timbers whose natural curves and bends matched the required shapes for both frames and strengthening components, such as knees which supported the deck beams. Axes and adzes were deftly used to sculpt the timbers to their perfect shape. Timbers were joined together by drilling holes and driving in either copper bolts or wooden trenails. Some timbers were seasoned, and the mast pond used for this purpose is one surviving feature of Portsmouth Dockyard. Planks were formed by splitting or sawing and then fitted to the frames. This construction method, called carvel, gave a smooth outer skin. Each plank was first held up to its neighbour so that shipwrights could then shape them to fit tightly together while following the curve of the side. Steaming made it easier to bend planks into position. Everything was made passably watertight by driving caulking, often made from unpicked rope, into the seams, and by tarring.

While the surviving hulls of shipwrecks often give the opportunity to study the work of shipwrights, rigging, which was the work of ropemakers, blockmakers and riggers, has usually been lost. However, Chatham Dockyard does have a display of rigging blocks, part of the large and unrivalled collection recovered from the wreck of HMS *Invincible*, which sank in 1758. Sailmakers also worked in large 'lofts'. Canvas of woven flax was supplied in broad cloths which had to be cut and sewn by hand to form huge sails. Their precise shape was essential to efficient sailing. The exact curvature of triangular fore and aft sails was achieved by joining variously shaped pieces known as gores. To allow sails to be hauled up and down, ropes were sewn to their edges and this had to allow for the differing degree of stretching or shrinking to be expected from hemp rope and canvas sail. Lighter cotton sails were only introduced to British vessels in the mid-nineteenth century. Sails for tall ships are still hand sewn, though for smaller vessels lighter sails of man-made fibres can be machined.

Ironwork was important to wooden boat and shipbuilding. Julius Caesar described iron bolts as thick as a man's thumb fastening the crossbeams of boats sailed in the Channel by Iron Age tribes of Britanny. Before carvel building was used in Northern Europe ships were built from the keel upwards by joining planks with their edges overlapping. They were commonly fastened by nails, sometimes called rivets, driven through from the outside and then bent over a washer-like rove. Frames were added afterwards, their outer faces knotched to fit over the stepped inside face of the so-called clinker planking. The largest clinker built vessel was the 175ft (53.3m) long *Grace Dieu*, laid down in 1416. Later carvel ships used iron knees, straps and eventually beams for strengthening. The ironwork from shipwrecks, attacked by seawater, is very difficult to stabilise. Often it has entirely corroded away and survives only as stains on adjoining wood or as rock-like concretions, which are formed from the decomposing metal and surrounding materials.

Julius Caesar also described the boats' iron chains and anchors. At that time, however, Mediterranean anchors were made of stone with holes cut for wooden tines. Stone anchors of this type have been found off Britain, notably some 20 examples from Poole Bay. Unfortunately it is not known if these undated finds were the work of local maritime manufacturers or from foreign ships.

Before the technology of casting was perfected in the late eighteenth century, iron anchors were forged from bundles of iron rods. This is apparent when forged anchors corrode, as they look grained like wood. Anchors large and small, from redundant ships and recovered from the seabed, have become a decorative motif of most coastal towns. In addition to full-size anchors some museum collections also include miniatures, often of brass, which were samples carried by salesmen.

49 Dry Dock, Gloucester with Eye of the Wind. *Dry docks became a feature of shipyards, especially for repair work. The vessel enters through lock-like gates on the high tide. Water drains out with the falling tide as the vessel is supported by props while her keel settles onto blocks. Gloucester Docks thrived by transhipping goods from the boats on the upper Severn to those using the estuary and Bristol Channel. The tall warehouses in the background were common on nineteenth-century waterfronts visited by small vessels whose cargo was manhandled in small units, such as sacks, barrels and bales. Regeneration of the docks has found new uses, including housing the National Waterways Museum*

50 Hydraulic crane, Leith

Between 1750 and 1790, the doubling of coal exports from the River Wear encouraged the growth of shipbuilding at Sunderland. By the end of the century there were around two dozen yards. In the age-old tradition of wooden shipbuilding they usually employed fewer than 30 men, and opened and closed with the fluctuating demand for ships. Shipwrights often joined informally with friends in a shipbuilding venture, acquiring timber on credit until the launch. It was common for the 'small' or waste timber from a ship under construction to be used simultaneously in building a smaller vessel alongside. By the 1830s capital investment had established some more permanent shipyards on the neighbouring Tyne. These typically had slipways, sail lofts, paint and joiners shops, sawmills, docks and even houses for the foremen. With 60 to 180 employees they built the highest class of vessels for foreign trades.

Permanent shipyards had also become a feature of smaller ports building far fewer vessels per year. These were often family businesses such as that set up by Thomas White.

51 Heavy Lift Crane (250 tonnes), Tyne 1993. With shipbuilding in decline companies diversified and this massive crane was retained to serve vessels visiting Newcastle's Offshore Technology Park. The small crane riding piggyback aids maintenance

52 Swan Hunter, Tyne. Heavy cranes and covered building areas characterised 1990s shipyards

After building ships on the beach at Broadstairs, Kent, around 1800 he took over an Isle of Wight shipyard in East Cowes. In 1815 he had opened Thetis Dock, a dry dock, capable of repairing East Indiamen. His investment proved wise since the dock was kept busy repairing ships damaged passing through the Channel thus saving them the cost and time of returning to large ports such as London.

The following decades saw advances in shipbuilding which changed shipyards and posed a challenge to builders of wooden ships in ports distant from the centres of industrial innovation. From the late eighteenth century pioneers had experimented with iron boats. By the 1830s shipbuilders on the Mersey, in Scotland and then on the Tyne began constructing iron hulls for sailing ships. By the 1850s the sailing ships were as large as 1000 tons, with iron giving the longitudinal strength combined with the lightness which had been so difficult to achieve with wooden framing. The early iron hulls were designed as those of wood using a half model to convey the final shape, but an additional plating model gave the details of every frame and plate to be manufactured. The construction process was similar but frames were jointed and plates formed into a skin by rivetting through ready-punched holes. The hearths, tongs and hammers of the rivetting teams are common museum exhibits. Those hand tools were only replaced by hydraulic rivetting tools in the 1880s, invented by R H Tweddell. The individual elements of an iron ship were cast and moulds of smaller components can also be found in museum collections.

The construction of metal hulls and fitting of engines increased the permanence of shipyards because capital investment was needed to provide the machinery which was increasingly essential. From the 1840s Armstrong's improvements enabled hydraulic power to be applied to cranes (**50**), capstans and dock gates. Large machines were needed to bend, punch and shear components of iron, and from the late 1870s steel. The modernisation of a shipyard in 1896, for Furness, Withy & Co in Hartlepool included installing a triple expansion steam engine to generate electricity, nine steam cranes and two steam hammers. Heavy lifting gear was needed to fit steam engines into ships, and the largest crane surviving beside the Tyne was originally used for this task (**51**).

The construction of iron ships focused on ports with ready access to raw materials: iron ore and minerals plus fuel for smelting, and coal to power the shipyard machinery. Existing technological know-how in ironworking and engine building were key factors, while the capacity for capital investment also dictated which ports made the most rapid advances. In this way shipbuilders on the Tyne began working in iron a good decade ahead of the smaller yards on the Wear. Despite excellent records in wooden ship construction, shipbuilders lacking the advantages of nearby materials, and specialist expertise had little hope of embracing large-scale iron shipbuilding. While the construction of the bulk of Britain's great merchant fleets centered on the North East and the Clyde, smaller shipbuilders survived by producing small wooden vessels or entering specialist markets by building yachts or small naval vessels, for example.

During the twentieth century the decline of British shipbuilding left derelict the riverfronts once lined with shipyards. It is a loss, like that of coal mining and fishing, keenly felt by communities which have built ships for generations. Amidst plans for regeneration and the boom in the heritage industry there were hopes of preserving a north east shipyard, but these have not come to fruition. Perhaps the scale of preservation was too great or perhaps there was just no political will. One candidate was Hebburn on the Tyne where, in the early 1990s, the gauntly empty brick workshops still crowded around the wet docks. Across the river Swan Hunters remained at work but under threat of closure. The construction process was concealed in great hangar-like ship sheds where draughtsman worked on computers, electronics guided the cutting of sheet metal and welders formed individual steel components which were brought together on the slipway. The most recently launched ship for the Royal Navy lay alongside with teams from the yard working aboard. As the Paddle Steamer Preservation Society's *Balmoral* steamed down the curiously quiet Tyne between the two yards her passengers spontaneously applauded the shipyard workers.

10 Watchers and waiters:
regulating the coast

> The coastline was the natural place for the authorities to try and tax the trade, or to stop it altogether. Being an island, Britain's borders are graphically defined.... The movement of goods across England's border was therefore an obvious business; the sails of a ship signalled its approach. Platt, 1991. *Smugglers' Britain*

Sea adventures, like all stories, grow in the telling. The exploits of sailors, who like Drake and Raleigh, have become national heroes, spin on the idea of valiant individuals defending their right to freedom on the high seas. In reality this freedom, *mare liberum*, was a cause championed by countries jealous of the commercial advantages won by rival maritime empires. More often than not the national interest was better served by claiming and exercising sovereignty over the seas, and this was most easily achieved around the home coast. Since merchant ships have always been vital to the economy and security of Britain, monarchs and governments have imposed regulations to control and guide their work with two main aims. The first was to raise revenue and the second to ensure that sufficient seamen and ships were available to defend the country. The capital value of cargoes and ships also created an interest in ensuring the safety of navigation.

Through the centuries close regulation of shipping and trade has been undertaken by diverse government departments and agencies, who employed large numbers of officials to watch the coast and wait upon unloading ships. Their work demanded meticulous record keeping and maritime historians can happily lose themselves in volumes of handwritten records which literally stretch for miles. Paperwork aside, the regulators have also left their mark on the coast.

HM Customs & Excise

As early as the tenth century trade attracted taxation when King Ethelred issued a list of cargoes, with corresponding fees to be paid in port. Their description as 'ancient customs' suggests such fees had been charged for a long time. After his conquest of England William I chose to collect the customs not in cash but by taking part of the cargo, a practice known as collecting prisage. It was Henry VII who set the customs on a regular footing by introducing a system called 'farming', in which individuals purchased the right to collect customs in return for an annual payment to the crown. During the thirteenth and fourteenth centuries sheep farming had become England's prime agricultural activity, and wool her major export. Once this export was taxed, smuggling of wools became a worthwhile business. In later centuries expanding trade extended the opportunities for taxation, particularly to raise revenue in time of war; the parallel increase in illegal imports and exports was countered by directing customs officers to actively combat smuggling. Whereas preventative work was coastwide their work as collectors was focused on the waterfronts of trading ports.

When Elizabethan maritime adventurers found new opportunities for trade across the world, the Queen saw the opportunity to maximise income from customs. Elizabeth revised the list of places where merchandise must be landed and adjusted the customs to be collected. Around these legal quays developed the ports which served into the industrial era. The legal quay in London was on the north of the Thames just below London Bridge. This part of the river, the Pool of London, remained the main point for landing goods until the construction of docks downriver in the late eighteenth century. The legal quay was 1,419ft (432m) in length. To cope with increased cargoes two sufferance quays were added: one of 2,890ft (881m) on the south bank below London Bridge, the other 790ft (241m) long, and situated below the Tower.

Smuggling received a fresh stimulus when William III increased customs to raise war finance. The system of farming had been replaced by the Board of Customs Commissioners in 1671 which appointed officers to collect the dues. Large numbers of officials were appointed as much to safeguard against corruption as to handle the volume of trade. Thus the Collector of Customs was overseen by the Controller and both were monitored by the Surveyor; under the eye of the tide-surveyor, tide-waiters boarded incoming vessels; land-surveyors oversaw coast-waiters and land-waiters who respectively supervised coastal and foreign cargoes; and searchers and weighers handled the goods.

Like collectors around the country, Robert Foxcroft and his miscellaneous staff in Lancaster, used a rented property on the legal quay until purpose-built premises were provided in 1762. Their Custom House, now opened as a local maritime museum, shows a typical layout. The ground floor provided storage for seized goods or waiting cargoes. The first floor comprised the Long Room, where merchants waited to be seen, with small offices and stores leading off. Merchants came to show their bills of lading which stated their cargo and how it was marked, the port of loading, the tonnage burthen of the ship, her owners and crew size.

Major ports built grandiose Custom Houses. After fire destroyed the old building London's new Custom House was given a Long Room measuring 190ft by 66ft and 55ft high (58m x 20m x 17m). The 1190ft (363m) long colonnaded river facade was added as part of building work after the Long Room collapsed into the warehouse below. More modest examples survive elsewhere, for example, at Exeter built about 1681 and Kings Lynn built in 1683. The Custom House at Poole (1813) stands near an original woolhouse (now the Waterfront Museum) and a reconstructed town beam whose steelyards once weighed commodities for customs to be calculated.

Expanding ports often sought the convenience and advantage of having their own Custom House and roused the rivalry of traditional custom ports. Greenock had competed with Port Glasgow for over a century before the Customs service was moved to the down river port. A new Custom House, designed by William Burn, was constructed between 1817 and 1819; the Long Room, complete with its wooden counter, is based on that designed by Christopher Wren for the seventeenth-century London Custom House. While the Excise Offices were housed in the east of the building the Customs Offices opened on to the riverfront, and this section of the building, including the Long Room, is now a HM Customs & Excise Museum.

A model of the large Customs House built at Liverpool as late as 1837, and demolished after war damage in 1943, is displayed in the HM Customs & Excise Museum within Merseyside Maritime Museum. From the mid-nineteenth century such grandiose buildings became less appropriate as the move from protectionist import duties to free trade reduced the need to accommodate waiting merchants and to store seized contraband, which meant that officials could be housed in smaller premises. In the twentieth century new forms of taxation, entry into the European Community and relaxation of border controls has again changed the workload. The HM Customs & Excise Museum stresses the high proportion of time given to VAT collection, and the emphasis on capture of illegal substances and control of counterfeit manufactures.

Coastguard

The history of the Coastguard is interwoven with the work of Customs authorities in preventing smuggling. The shore-based service can be traced back to 1698, when, faced with an increase in smuggling, William III hired fast smacks to chase smuggling boats and established armed riding officers to patrol the coast.

In 1809 a Preventative Water Guard was established. Based in some 150 coastal stations, their facilities amounted to watchhouses and boathouses for their shore-based boats. Six years later the war against Napoleon ended and the Admiralty, which faced the unpalatable task of reducing the navy to peace-time force, decided to create a naval reserve by placing both ships and men at the disposal of the Customs. Twelve hundred men were directed to this Coast Blockade which initially covered the coast of Kent but was later extended nationwide. While some personnel were accommodated afloat or in derelict ships many were billeted in existing coastal buildings such as the defensive Martello towers.

By 1822 the force was being called the Coast Guard and had expanded to some 3000 men. Throughout the nineteenth century responsibility and funding for the service continued to move between the Admiralty, Board of Trade and Customs & Excise. Accommodation was a key issue. To live within a local community brought the risk of officers succumbing to bribery and corruption; at the other end of the scale hostility and ostracism often left coastguards unable to find lodgings. Preventative Stations with living quarters for men and officers were the solution (**53**). At Lymington, Hampshire, for example, the Coast Guard took over No.3 Dukes Head Cottages from the Customs Collector. After 1869 there was a move towards buying accommodation and the cost of over 500 stations was estimated at £20,000.

By the twentieth century there were 4000 Coast Guards fulfilling a diverse role

53 Lepe Coastguard Houses (1850s) are typically located to overlook a popular smuggling route. Any boat approaching the quiet Beaulieu River would have to pass close inland under the windows of the watch house on the shore

including: the prevention of smuggling; collecting shipping statistics; registering fishing vessels; and lifesaving. The deployment of life-saving apparatus to rescue crews from wrecked ships had also mobilised a massive volunteer force, which is described in the next chapter. A review in 1922 re-established the service as the Coastguard and rationalised its responsibilities. Over the next fourteen years the Office of Works improved and acquired new accommodation for the Coastguard providing more than 250 stations with a further 750 auxiliary stations by the mid-1930s.

The modern Coastguard is solely responsible for coordinating search and rescue. They operate far fewer coastal stations since technology such as radar and satellite navigation has improved ship safety; radio and telephones enable rapid communication and response; and rescue is now achieved off-shore by helicopters and long-range lifeboats. Rationalisation of the service has left some lookouts redundant. Some of these are now used by a voluntary organisation the National Coastwatch Institute.

While smuggling and shipwrecks are a feature of many local museums far less emphasis falls on the long and diverse work of the Coastguard, although there is a National Coastguard Museum at Bridlington in Yorkshire. In addition modern walkers are preserving an intangible part of the Coastguards' work by literally following in their footsteps. For much of its 594-mile (956km) route, the South West Coast Path (Minehead, Somerset to near Poole, Dorset) follows the path patrolled daily by coastguards until 1913. Many of the country's other cliff-top paths lead walkers past headland lookouts and distinctive rows of Coastguard cottages (**58**).

Trinity Houses

Medieval guilds provided status and self-regulation for skilled craftsman. Seaman from individual ports formed fraternities or guilds with charitable aims, such as supporting retired mariners and their widows and orphans, and which took responsibility for maritime matters such as regulating pilots, providing buoys and beacons, and setting standards in the education of seamen.

In 1514 Henry VIII granted a charter to the Guild of Holy Trinity and St Clement, an organisation which had controlled pilots on the Thames for several centuries. From this organisation evolved the Corporation of Trinity House, Deptford to which Elizabeth I granted the right to erect 'Beakons Markes and Signes for the Sea'. Similarly, Trinity House, Newcastle, originated as the medieval Guild of Masters and Mariners, occupying premises in Broad Chare from 1505. An adjacent building now houses a museum: the Trinity Maritime Centre. Likewise, Trinity House, Leith, was built in 1817 on a site in Kirkgate which the organisation, originally called the Fraternity, had occupied since the sixteenth century. Parallel organisations developed in other major ports, including: Trinity House, Hull; the Society of Merchant Venturers, Bristol; and the Company of Pilots, Dover.

Besides their surviving administrative houses, their work has left few physical remains with the exception of the many lighthouses marking the port entrances and hazards on the main trade routes. The right to erect a lighthouse was traditionally purchased in the form of a patent from the crown. Not until 1836 was Trinity House, Deptford, given authority to purchase all existing patents and take responsibility for lights throughout England and Wales. Five years later, in 1841, it cost £444,984 to purchase the last from private control. This was the Skerries, a rocky islet off Anglesey, which lay on the busy and therefore lucrative shipping lanes to Liverpool. Since 1786 Scottish lighthouses have been built and maintained by the Commissioners of Northern Lights, who also have responsibility for lighthouses in the Isle of Man.

Lighthouses

The fascination of lighthouses must be attributed to their construction marking man's triumph against the power of nature. Rising with perfect symmetry from rocks in the wild sea these awesome, solitary towers mark the unrivalled engineering skills of their architects and the hardiness of their builders. They are no less monuments to the fiscal and administrative capabilities of the great trading empires which constructed them. Pharology, the study of lighthouses, takes its name from the Pharos of Alexandria, one of the seven wonders of the ancient world. This 466ft (142m) high lighthouse was built around 280BC and represented the might, wealth and vision of a trading empire based on the fertile Nile.

The oldest surviving lighthouse in Britain was built by imperial Rome, whose trade network drew commodities from these offshore islands including tin and slaves. The 79ft (24m) high octagonal stone lighthouse on the cliffs above Dover might have guided

54 St Aldhelm's Chapel. From the roof of this stoutly built chapel a fire burned to guide seamen past the turbulent waters off St Albans head. A more recent Coastguard look out perches on the very edge of the cliff (far right)

shipping or aided the channel fleet, the *Classis Britannica*, in keeping the route to Europe free from pirates. The surviving lighthouse now stands inside Dover Castle and the base of a second exists on the Western Heights. Lights may also have been shown from signal stations set up on main sea routes. Surviving remains are found at Filey Brigg and Scarborough, North Yorkshire, and on Steep Holm in the Bristol Channel.

While histories of lighthouse buildings often make the unlikely leap from the Dover pharos to eleventh-century chapels there is no reason to suppose an entire lack of navigation aids in the intervening centuries. Indeed excavated charcoal at Bamburgh, Northumberland, has been interpreted as the remains of a beacon. In darkness a light would identify the stark rock outcrop, now topped by Bamburgh Castle, which remains a day-time landmark for coastal shipping.

Legend attributes the construction around 1140 of the chapel on St Aldhelm's Head, Dorset (**54**), to a father whose daughter and son-in-law were lost in the maelstrom 350ft (108m) below. Written records confirm its presence in the following century and later service as a seamark while modern repairs have revealed evidence that a beacon was indeed kept alight on its roof. Documents record how a surviving purpose-built lighthouse was erected in the 1320s through the medieval equivalent of today's Community Service. Walter de Godeton had pillaged the cargo of a ship wrecked on the Isle of Wight. As punishment he was ordered to provide and maintain a lighthouse. His octagonal stone tower can be visited on the hill above Blackgang. Unlike many medieval lights its fire was inside the tower's top and shone through eight glazed windows which formed the lantern. The small windows and low fog meant the light was of little use and its replacement, St Catherine's lighthouse built in 1838, stands on the undercliff. In 1875 even this tower was

55 *North Shields Low Light (1805) from the High Light. Similarly aligning the lights from seaward provided ships with safe route into the Tyne. The breakwaters were not built until late in the nineteenth century*

reduced in height to increase the effectiveness of the light. In poor visibility foghorns became a vital substitute (**colour plate 15**).

Warning lights also burned from prominent coastal buildings including Tynemouth Priory, Tyne & Wear, and Orford Castle, Suffolk. In the medieval period religious orders and castle-based lords were the only people with the ability to acquire regular supplies of wood or coal and sufficient manpower to keep the lights burning. Their motives may have been as much self-serving as altruistic. The Prior of Tynemouth, for example, was shipping coal out of the Tyne and a shipwreck would have been a costly accident. Lighthouse building also attracted entrepreneurs. Having invested in building and keeping a light, a businessman could, with permission from the Crown, charge a fee to passing ships. Known as lightage, this was collected at the nearest port.

In 1536 a charter from Henry VIII gave Trinity House, Newcastle, permission to build both a high and a low light at North Shields. When an approaching ship saw these two lights in line its course was right for entering the shoal mouth of the Tyne. These are the first recorded example of leading lights. The original lights were stone-built and glazed to protect the candles from draughts. In 1658 shifting sandbanks forced Trinity House to realign the lights, by building new wooden towers. The present towers were built in 1805 (**55**).

Advances in lighthouse design and construction centred on the challenge of marking offshore reefs and rocks. The first successful rock lighthouse was erected off Cornwall on the awesome triple reef, called Eddystone, by Henry Winstanley. Starting in 1696 it took three seasons to set 12 iron stanchions into the rock, lay a solid base of stone 16ft (4.86m) in diameter, and complete the 80ft high (24.4m) tower and lantern above. The project showed the difficulties that would face future builders along Britain's Atlantic swept coast. The reef presented a 30-degree slope and on a high spring tide only 3ft (0.9m) of the rock was uncovered. On some days no more than two hours work was achieved on the rock. After a nine hour row from Plymouth labourers worked with hand tools in drenching salt spray, and all the building stone had to be manhandled from open boats onto the slippery rocks.

The 60 candles of the first Eddystone light were lit in November 1698. By the following year the cement joints had been dangerously eroded. Winstanley encased the base and tower in fresh masonry and protected the new joints with bands of iron. After five years of successfully warning shipping this improved tower was among the maritime casualties of the extraordinarily severe Great Storm of November 1703. Only the iron stanchions remained after the storm.

Winstanley's tower was replaced by a stone and timber lighthouse which burnt down in 1755. When John Smeaton then built the third Eddystone lighthouse his innovation set the pattern for future tower construction. The central masonry blocks of the base were dovetailed into the rock itself and interlocked with their neighbours, while marble dowels secured the courses together. Stability was improved by tapering the tower to give a lower centre of gravity. After James Douglass built a replacement in 1882, the Smeaton lighthouse was moved to Plymouth Hoe, where it can still be visited.

Fewer than 10 rock lighthouses existed by the end of the eighteenth century. Construction then quickened under the lighthouse authorities, and just as in other fields of Victorian engineering, lighthouse building became a family affair: generations of Stevensons served the Northern Lighthouse Board and the Douglass family worked for Trinity House.

Robert Stevenson improved on Smeaton's ideas. He completed the 100ft (30.4m) high Bell Rock Lighthouse in 1810, having used dovetailing throughout every course of masonry. Perched on a rock 12 miles off Arbroath, Tayside, it was vital to maximise working time during construction. This was achieved by first building an offshore barracks where the workforce could safely rest during high tides and storms.

The lighthouse keepers were supported from a complex in Arbroath, which is now a museum. Relief keepers lived here with their families, and used the signal tower to maintain daily communication with the lighthouse. Land based lighthouses were also built with adjoining houses for families, together with a parcel of land where food could be grown. This type of arrangement is opened to the public by the National Trust at Souter Point Lighthouse on the coast of Tyne and Wear (**56**).

Cast iron was the wonder material of the early nineteenth century and its champions believed it would provide a quick and cheap method of lighthouse construction. It was used for a harbour light at Swansea in 1803, and first tried in an offshore lighthouse at Maplin Sands, Essex in 1838. It was soon found, however, that cast iron structures were insufficiently robust for rock lighthouses, the most exposed locations. One of the few surviving cast iron lighthouses can be seen in Cliff Park, Roker, Sunderland. The 50ft (15.2m) high tower was built in 1856 by Thomas Meek and originally stood at the mouth

56 *Souter Lighthouse, Tyne & Wear was operational 1871-1988. Now a National Trust property it comprises both the lighthouse tower and surrounding complex of buildings which include the living accommodation of keepers and their families*

of the River Wear on the end of the South Pier.

Working on the Welsh and Cornish coast the Douglass family sought a solution to the problem of huge waves surging up the walls of lighthouse towers. In the 1850s James Walker had designed a stepped base for the Smalls Lighthouse, Dyfed, which broke up the waves. When constructing the Bishop Rock Lighthouse, on the extreme west of the Isles of Scilly, James Douglass improved on Walker's design by encasing the tower's base in a masonry drum, 41ft (12.5m) in diameter and 38ft (11.6m) high. This became common practice.

Providing a constant clear light while minimising the risk of fire was as important a logistical challenge as constructing the lighthouse tower. Open fires were commonly used in the eighteenth century and were seen last at St Bees Lighthouse, Cumbria in 1823. Using high quality coal they could be visible from a distance of 7 miles (11.3km). Candles and reflectors were commonly used in leading lights. Medieval cressets had comprised hollowed-out stone filled with oil or fat which burnt via a wick. In 1784 a reliable, fuel-efficient oil lamp was developed by Ami Argand and this became common in nineteenth-century lighthouses with both whale and herring oil among the fuels used. Oil lamps were greatly improved by the introduction of paraffin in the 1860s. Glazed lanterns protected the lights from wind and rain. Late in the eighteenth century parabolic reflectors were used to concentrate the light into a beam. This effect was improved in 1822 when Augustin Fresnel developed an annular lens which comprised a central section surrounded by concentric rings; this concentrated the light. With the lens now set in front of the light source further improvements were achieved using refraction.

In 1862, steam engines generated electricity to power the light at Dungeness. In 1922 South Foreland was lit using mains electricity and in the same year the Trwyn Du,

57 From 1853 Time Ball Tower, Deal. Daily at noon an electric signal from Greenwich raised and dropped the balls as a visual time checks for ships anchored in the Downs. The paved seating area by the tower is furnished with an anchor, the ubiquitous maritime motif of the modern seafront

Anglesey, became the first fully-automated lighthouse. As recently as 1982, Eddystone became the first offshore lighthouse to be fully automated, and it was only a matter of time before all lights could be kept without being manned. As lighthouses have been upgraded and automated, their optics, lamps and machinery have become a feature of many coastal museums.

Time and navigation

While lighthouses and seamarks assisted ships making coastal voyages, buildings were also set up to assist the deep-sea navigator. Out of sight of land, ships' positions were plotted by measuring latitude and longitude but the latter could only be found with the use of an accurate timepiece, or chronometer. From 1833 the Royal Observatory at Greenwich marked 12.00 noon by raising and dropping a timeball, whose fall could be seen by ships on the Thames. The site of a timeball on the Tyne was lost when ballast mounds were cleared, while at Bidston, Birkenhead, a modern observatory occupies the hilltop where the Mersey's timeball once stood. A timeball tower survives, however, on the seafront in Deal, Kent, and has opened as a museum since 1985 (**57**). It was built in 1795 as a shutter telegraph station to serve ships in the Downs anchorage. Messages reached London in two minutes via fifteen stations. In 1853 it was converted to a timeball station, and the signal to operate the ball's descent was passed by an electric current directly from Greenwich. The station was closed in 1927 by which time wireless was in use.

11   Lifesaving

> It drives on with a courage which is stronger than the storm. It drives on with
> a mercy which does not quail in the presence of death. It drives on as proof, a
> symbol, a testimony that man is created in the image of God and that valour
> and virtue have not perished in the British race. Winston Churchill

For 200 years lifeboatmen have been volunteers: ordinary men from local ports, harbours
and fishing villages. Their heroism was succoured by their families and neighbours who
raised the money to purchase and maintain the boats, and who physically launched them
and then anxiously watched and waited to safely beach them on their return. Lifesaving
was a community affair. Its moments of high achievement and of sad failure are emotively
etched in family and local history. Physical reminders of past rescues often take on the
status of memorials held in the custody of local people. At the same time the
determination to provide today's lifesavers with the greatest chance of returning safely
from successful rescues means that their equipment must be constantly upgraded. New
lifeboat designs have demanded alterations to lifeboat houses, which have been
longstanding features of harbours and beaches, while the deployment of fast long-range
vessels has left other houses redundant. Improvements in navigation aids, vessel safety and
rescue techniques has brought the demise of other life-saving services, so committing
their shoreside facilities to history.

The Royal National Lifeboat Institution now intend their high-speed lifeboats to be
able to reach a vessel 50 miles off the coast in just two and half hours. Just a century earlier,
before radio communication, it was usually impossible for stricken vessels to seek
assistance unless they were in sight of land. In fog, rain or darkness they were often not
sighted until they were aground on sandbanks, rocks or beneath cliffs. For this reason,
early attempts to organise rescues focused as much on inventing mortars or rockets to
throw lines from shore to ship as on building boats for lifesaving.

In 1791 John Bell was awarded £50 by the Society for the Encouragement of Arts,
Manufacture and Commerce for inventing a mortar which could fire a line from a ship to
the shore. More than twenty years passed before such equipment was successful in a real
life rescue. Captain George Manby used a mortar to fire a line to the Sunderland collier
Nancy which had been driven onto the Norfolk coast. A small boat was then hauled back
and forth to bring her crew ashore. Manby refined this equipment by designing a small
cradle to replace the boat. His Life Saving Apparatus (LSA) came in three weights for
transport by man, horse or cart (**58**).

In 1829 the Coast Guard Service was issued with Manby's LSA, equipment which
would still have been recognised by a Coastguard in the 1970s. It used mortars to carry a

58 *Coastguards role in lifesaving made it vital to locate stations, like this on St Albans Head, Dorset, close to treacherous reefs and lee shores which frequently wrecked ships. Sheds were provided to house the LSA cart*

light line over the ship and a hawser which was pulled onto the ship using the light line. Once the hawser was secure a travelling block was set on it, from which was suspended a kismee buoy. The kismee buoy was pulled backwards and forwards from the ship on an endless rope, using lines called whips. The kit also included tally boards bearing instructions on how to use the LSA. With the plight of foreign crews in mind each board had instructions in English, French, Dutch and German. A later addition was the hawser-cutting block. With everyone safely ashore, the kismee buoy was taken down and the cutting block substituted. It was pulled to the ship where its blades severed the expensive hawser which could then be hauled in. The mortars were soon surpassed by rockets, invented by John Dennett, which were easier to carry and more accurate. Coast Guard equipment was then upgraded with Boxer Rockets in the 1860s. These were only replaced after the Second World War when the Ministry of Defence developed an electrically ignited rocket.

In 1864 a shipwreck in the north east changed the face of shore-to-ship rescue. In bad weather the steamship *Stanley* sought shelter in the River Tyne. She was caught by heavy seas in the river entrance (**55**) and driven north onto notorious rocks called the Black Middens. On that November day the weather was wreaking havoc in the busy river. Even if the four local lifeboats had not already been at work taking crews from stranded sailing vessels, the shallow water would have prevented them reaching *Stanley*. Crowds gathered as the Tynemouth Coast Guards struggled in strong winds to set up their LSA and begin hauling people to safety. When two of the first four brought ashore died many of their fellow passengers were afraid to make the same perilous journey over jagged rocks pounded by breaking waves. Then the lines of the LSA jammed, halting the rescue until

59 Tynemouth Volunteer Life Brigade Watch House (1866) where members keep alive the tradition of volunteer lifesaving and preserve historic life saving apparatus used in ship to shore rescues

runners could fetch new equipment from nearby Cullercoats. The shoreside crowd was helpless as they watched *Stanley* break in two, spilling five crew and twenty passengers into the murderous seas at a spot which you can overlook today from the river promenade beneath Tynemouth.

Sensing the shock caused by the wreck, the Mayor of Tynemouth called a public meeting to suggest that local people could be trained to assist the Coast Guard. Two hundred and twenty members joined the new Tynemouth Volunteer Life Brigade (VLB). It was endorsed and equipped by the Board of Trade and trained by the Coast Guard. The VLB still occupies its wooden Watch House built in 1866 (**59**). This is a distinctive landmark above the Tyne with white painted and glazed towers. The Watch House retains sets of LSA from all eras and a wealth of memorabilia from shipwrecks, rescues and brigade members.

The VLB idea spread like fire around the coast. In 1913 there were some 5000 members in over four hundred brigades. By this date merchant vessels were larger and so less numerous. The proportion of engined ships was also far higher, and they had greater ability to avoid tides and winds driving them ashore. Consequently LSA was needed for fewer rescues and the numbers of VLB fell, reaching 261 by 1924. The rationalised Coastguard now had rescue as its primary task and a Coast Life-Saving Corps was formed to pull the two organisations together. With many VLBs absorbed into the Corps, their independence was further reduced by creation of the Auxiliary Coastguard in 1964. With improved technology the need for shore-to-ship rescues was becoming negligible and, in

1988, the Coastguard withdrew LSA.

The only surviving VLBs are Tynemouth, South Shields formed in 1866, and Sunderland formed in 1877. The South Shields Watch House, built of wood in 1876, stands at the landward end of the South Pier. Its octagonal watchtower gives a clear view of the two points where many ships came to grief: the outside of the pier and, inside, the sands running north to the Groyne Light. Sunderland VLB was divided into several brigades. Their brick-built Roker Watch House (1906) overlooks the River Wear from the top of Pier View Road. A small stone watchhouse also stands on the cliff edge above Cullercoats Bay, Tyne & Wear while a garage across the road once housed the LSA. Another stone watch house survives at Seaton Sluice, Northumberland (**11**).

Elsewhere on the coast there is little to remember the shoreside lifesavers except where their own communities have preserved some memento. In the Ship Inn at Seahouses, Northumberland, for example, space was found for the webbing belts whose numbers denote the place of each local VLB member in the LSA drill.

The North East also played a key role in initiating lifeboat stations. As early as the 1780s a Northumbrian cleric pursued the idea of converting a local coble into a lifeboat for Bamburgh. He approached a London coachbuilder, Lionel Lukin, who had already created an 'unsinkable boat' by giving a cork belt to a Norway yawl. While the outcome of this initiative is uncertain, a buoyant cork belt was to be a feature of the boat design which became synonymous with lifeboats on the Tyne, Wear, Tees and beyond.

In the same way that tragedy spawned the Volunteer Life Brigades, it was a wreck that precipitated the construction of the North East's most famous lifeboat. On 14 March 1789 a fleet of colliers returning to the Tyne was met by a northerly gale and the *Adventure* missed the entrance to the river. Her crew battled for more than 24 hours to carry her over the shallow bar but were eventually driven onto Herd Sands. The fishermen of South Shields had often rescued crews from the many ships which grounded on these banks but even they could not launch their cobles through the tremendous surf. *Adventure* was smashed to pieces. Only five of her 13 crew survived, clinging to wreckage which washed ashore.

The local shipowners offered a prize of two guineas for a model of a boat which could be launched into high waves for the purpose of saving lives. In a strange twist they denied the winner, William Wouldhave, his prize; then modified the design and chose Henry Greathead as builder. The 28ft 6in (8.7m) *Original* was stationed at South Shields. She was built of clinker planks and was double-ended with a sharp bow and stern. Her keel curved and she had a cork belt below the gunwale.

The oldest surviving lifeboat in Britain is *Zetland* built by Greathead in 1802. When the RNLI supplied a new lifeboat the people of Redcar, Cleveland, saved *Zetland* from burning. After decades ashore she was hurriedly launched, rowing to a shipwreck to which the RNLI boat could not return because she was too badly damaged when beaching with survivors. Approaching her 200th birthday *Zetland* is now at home to visitors on the seafront at Redcar. Instead of being transferred to a museum she has remained in her boathouse, originally built for the lifeboat *Emma* in 1877, which was taken over for *Zetland* in 1969. Her fine appearance owes much to remaining in the sea air, which has always surrounded her, and to the volunteers who tend her.

For over a century South Shields has also marked its bond with lifesaving by preserving a Greathead-type lifeboat. After 60 years on station the lifeboat *Tyne*, built by Oliver in 1833, was towed over the steep hill from her riverside boathouse and set up on Marine Parade (**60**). A third Greathead-type, *Bedford* (1885) also from the Tyne station, was in the marvellous international boat collection gathered by David Goddard at the Exeter Maritime Museum, now transferred to Great Yarmouth, Norfolk.

While the *Original* is often considered to be the first lifeboat other ports responded similarly to the dreadful loss of local ships and men, and Liverpool is also among those claiming to have the earliest lifeboat. There is no doubt, however, that Greathead lifeboats were the first to be stationed on many parts of the coast. Using a standard design, he constructed more than 20 for British stations and also sent them overseas. Builders in Sunderland and Hartlepool also supplied lifeboats using the Greathead design. Since each lifeboat was operated independently shoreside facilities varied from place to place and it was often a struggle to maintain stations. A committee of local subscribers in Montrose, for example, purchased a Greathead lifeboat in 1807 as a replacement for their existing boat. After a decade the Committee was in debt and asked the Town Council to take over the lifeboat. Eventually, in 1819, an independently elected body, the Harbour Lights Committee, assumed responsibility. They built a shed for the lifeboat next to the port's lower leading light.

Sir William Hillary who crewed an Isle of Man lifeboat, used the national press to highlight the need for a well-funded coastwide service. In 1824 his vision produced the National Institution for the Preservation of Life from Shipwreck. In 1854 this became the National Lifeboat Institution, which with the consent of Queen Victoria soon took the title Royal National Lifeboat Institution.

The RNLI has just celebrated its 175th anniversary as a volunteer organisation. Its members have a strong sense of history, and preserved lifeboats must rank as one of the most numerous historical maritime objects. On decommissioning many have gone into mufti as fishing and pleasure craft. Others are designer heritage icons set up on modern maritime developments such as riverside walks and yacht harbours; one such is the 48' Oakley class *Arthur and Ruby Reed* (1966), once stationed at Cromer, Norfolk, and now mounted alongside Hythe marina in Hampshire (**61**). Of the older survivors, a few are restored to working order like the *Victoria* (1889), believed to be the oldest RNLI boat afloat. Some are pristine exhibits, often in their original boathouses, such as RNLB *Robert & Ellen Robinson* at Whitby, the last pulling and sailing lifeboat to be withdrawn from service.

It is difficult to define the force which drives communities and individuals to preserve these vessels. Undoubtedly its core lies in the imagery of the lifeboat, the essence of which was captured by Winston Churchill in the words quoted at the opening of this chapter. However enthralled they might be by the drama of the lifeboat's launch, rescue and recovery most people would not so much as turn to look at the humble, functional lifeboat house. Yet these are equally part of the RNLI's history. Many survive, disused or reused, where the lifeboats are long gone. Their design has made possible the maintenance and launch of lifeboats on every part of Britain's diverse coast with sound construction ensuring their longevity in some of the most exposed and inhospitable

60 *The Greathead-type
lifeboat* Tyne *(1833)
at South Shields. The
creation of this
maritime memorial
from their recently
decommissioned
lifeboat signifies the
strong bond between
the 1890s towns
people and lifesaving.*
Tyne *herself is
double-ended, built of
clinker planking, with
a broad cork belt
beneath the gunwale.
Thole pins mark the
position of five pairs of
oarsmen; the eleventh
steered from either
stern or stem*

locations. The power of the elements was demonstrated at Porthleven, Cornwall, where the original lifeboat house was built on rocks on the seashore. A severe gale stove in the doors, and the waves which rushed inside forced the lifeboat through the roof of its house.

Back in the late 1840s the organisation was at a low ebb until its fortunes were revived under the Presidency of the Duke of Northumberland. Following another design competition the Institution agreed its first standard lifeboat. This was a double-ended 30ft (9m) long boat, large enough to carry sixty people and was either pulled by ten oars or sailed. The development of a standard design should have brought uniformity to the specification for RNLI boathouses. However, the lifeboats were modified to cope with specific launch and sea conditions and the boathouses were similarly constructed to suit local environments.

The Yorkshire coast, for example, has no natural harbour between the broad Tees Estuary and the River Esk at Whitby. To provide a lifeboat station the RNLI squeezed a boathouse between the cliff and river at Staithes. The house had to face the village rather than the open sea and was originally provided with a unique curving slipway. The house is now protected as a Listed Building. At Aldeburgh, Suffolk, no lifeboat house was provided. The boat was kept instead on a raised plinth and launched down the steep shingle beach. Llandudno in Gwynedd lies at the foot of the Great Orme peninsula with sea on two sides of the town, so the 1903 lifeboat house was placed halfway between the North and West Shores. Horses originally pulled the lifeboat to the sea on either side. Since construction of a seawall to the west modern launches always take place to the east,

61 Oakley Class lifeboat, Hythe. In contrast to Tyne, *the* Arthur & Ruby Reed *has been removed from her station and community to decorate a marina development. Excellent product placement for the RNLI which depends on voluntary subscriptions to maintain a now coastwide service whose rescues are increasingly of those sailing for leisure*

and holiday traffic has to stop as the landrover or tractor draws the boat through the town. The Bristol Channel has a huge tidal range, and at low tide buildings on the seafront are many metres from the waters edge. At Weston-Super-Mare the present lifeboat station is on Birnbeck Island which is reached via the town pier. From here a slipway launches the lifeboat safely into the water whatever the state of the tide, despite the 43ft (13m) difference between high and low water.

Many surviving lifeboat houses are proof of Victorian design and engineering skills. From the mid-nineteenth century Charles Henry Cooke served as Honorary Architect to the RNLI. In three decades he oversaw the construction of more than two-hundred lifeboat houses, which continued to shelter wooden, pulling and sailing lifeboats well into the twentieth century. While RNLI boat designs were continually reviewed they did not undergo the change in scale and materials imposed on merchant ships by the introduction of iron, and then steel hulls. Instead lifeboats used a construction technique advanced by wooden shipbuilders in the 1850s and '60s to compete with the lightness and strength of metal hulls. Double or triple skins of thin planks laid diagonally provided great strength and reduced the need for bulky internal framing. Pulling lifeboats increased to 38ft (11.6m) in length and sailing boats to 41ft (12.5m). Between 1888 and 1901 the RNLI experimented with steam propulsion, as engined lifeboats would have great advantages in adverse winds and for towing. However the engines did not find favour and only six steam lifeboats were commissioned.

The initial adoption of motor engines for lifeboats brought little modification to the lifeboat houses. Although by 1914 there were 21 motor lifeboats on station their engines initially provided only a supplement to the sails and oars. Attention was also given to making engined lifeboats light enough to continue their traditional launching from open beaches. The last pulling and sailing lifeboat was decommissioned as late as 1956. During the transition to motorised lifeboats, the work of Cooke was continued by the RNLI architect W T Douglass who established lifeboat houses which, with little change, served the Institution from 1940 to 1980. In the later decades the working life of some shoreside facilities was prolonged by thoughtful planning, such as the design specification for the new Tyne class lifeboats which actually included the requirement that they should fit existing boathouses.

During the twentieth century improvements in ship navigation and safety and the construction of high-powered lifeboats with greater range have enabled a reduction and rationalisation in the number of lifeboat stations. The robust lifeboat houses often find new uses. At Hunstanton, Norfolk, the present lifeboat house, originally built in 1867, was a fisherman's store from 1931 to 1979. At Porthleven, Cornwall, the lifeboat house at the harbour entrance is now a dive school. The old lifeboat house for Rye stands isolated on the bleak shingle ridges behind the beach to the west of the River Rother. This was the home of the pulling boat *Mary Stanford* which capsized with all hands in 1928. In the local churchyard, above the graves of the 17 crew, is the inscription 'We have done that which was our duty to do'. The modern lifeboat house, unusually painted blue and white, now stands in Rye Harbour itself.

Tenby, Dyfed, is among the stations where changing launches can be traced through a series of surviving lifeboat houses. Old Ordnance Survey maps show the first on the quayside where it now serves as an unremarkable lock-up building, tucked in the corner of the harbour. From 1852 it housed a boat supplied by the Shipwrecked Fishermen's & Mariners' Royal Benevolent Society. At low tide the harbour dries and the lifeboat would have to be hauled beyond the harbour piers to reach the waters edge. Once afloat it would still have to round the castle promontory. In 1862 the RNLI housed a new boat in a purpose-built lifeboat house on Castle Sands. It was replaced in 1895 by a boathouse, built of rusticated stone, which stands at the entrance to the beach. Sheltered by St Margarets Island but otherwise facing the open sea, its former use is betrayed by double doors to seaward and the remains of a small slip. Ten years later the difficulties of a 28ft (8.5m) tidal range were overcome by placing a lifeboat house high on the cliff promontory beside the castle with a 360ft (109.7m) long launching slipway constructed with iron piles in the tradition of pier building (**62**). Modifications and repairs have prepared this lifeboat house for service into the twenty-first century.

During the last decade of the twentieth century the upgrading of lifeboat houses around the country has amounted to one of the most intensive building and civil engineering phases in the RNLI's history. The especially appointed Shoreworks Engineer Howard Ritchie was expected to provide crew facilities such as toilets and showers which were missing from the older stations; meet the needs of new and larger boat designs; and cope with the complexities of a perpetually changing coast where erosion threatens many waterfront buildings. The history and tradition of the RNLI has confronted him with an additional challenge. When built, most working lifeboat houses stood on beaches littered

62 Tenby Lifeboat house, Dyfed. The slipway supported on metal piles overcomes the difficulties of a 28ft tidal range. The first lifeboat house was at the back of the harbour, far right, and had to be dragged across the sand at low water

with the paraphernalia of inshore fishing boats, in busy fishing or trading harbours, or on lonely stretches of open coast. These environments have changed as today, tourism rather than maritime activity sustains many of Britain's seaboard communities. Now the lifeboat houses are important features on popular seafronts, in picturesque harbours and beside coastal paths. Their historic character has been recognised and several have been given legal protection either as Listed Buildings or as part of Conservation Areas. Howard Ritchie has had to achieve modernisation while preserving the appearance of the original lifeboat houses.

Upgrading of the Cullercoats station, Northumberland, left unaltered the ornate gable ends, barge boards and bell tower. This 1896 lifeboat house carries the inscription: 'So when they cry unto the Lord in their trouble he delivereth them of their distress and bringeth them into the haven where they would be'. At North Sunderland, also in Northumberland, the boathouse is of functional design built of modern materials. However, it has been clad with stone to blend in with the architecture of Seahouses Harbour. At Filey, North Yorkshire, the boathouse was rebuilt in 1991 but, despite losing the arched doorway, the brick facade as far as possible replicates the 1889 original. This has maintained the character of the seafront. The lifeboat house at Walmer, Kent is sited on the beach and has an unusual appearance with flying buttresses. In 1991 the front of the building was taken down and re-erected nearly 6m (20ft) to seaward. This provided space for a larger boat, the Atlantic 21, without altering the appearance of the building. Hastings lifeboat house is on the beach in front of the Old Town adjacent to the net shops where tourists visit the nearby Fishing Museum, aquarium or Shipwreck Heritage Centre. By lowering the floor a new lifeboat was accommodated without external alterations to the boathouse.

Elsewhere entirely new structures have been introduced. In contrast to Hastings, at Aldeburgh, Suffolk, a new lifeboat house has provided the necessary 62ft (19m) for the same Mersea Class lifeboat and its launching tractor and trailor. The controversial design

63 Staithes Lifeboat house. The crews all-in-one waterproof suits hang beneath the service boards which record rescues made by their predecessors who put to sea in heavy leather boots, knitted jumpers, oilskins, and cork lifebelts

consists of a boathouse suspended from an external stainless steel A-frame. The foundations are protected by sheet-piling as, despite build up of shingle, the East Anglia coastline is also vulnerable to sudden erosion. The increase in watersports has been matched by the provision of fast, inshore rescue boats. In the sheltered water at Burnham, Essex, in Brighton Marina, East Sussex, and in Poole Harbour, Dorset, these have been provided with a totally new design of floating lifeboat house alongside pontoon-type jetties. Once inside, the boats are raised from the water on a hinged platform while crew facilities have to be provided ashore.

Many working lifeboat houses are opened to the public. Elsewhere disused or reused boathouses may have lost their significance, but lifeboat mementos are kept as reminders of the service of men bound to the sea. Where stations have closed their service boards, recording each launch and rescue, have often found homes in other local buildings.

Unfortunately Rye is not alone in having lost her lifeboat crew. With family members volunteering side by side lifeboat losses, like those in fishing fleets, cut through small communities. Here memorials mark not just their service but their sacrifice. The church above Mousehole, Cornwall, holds such a poignant and fitting memorial. A huge sea-smoothed granite boulder commemorates the eight-man crew of the Penlee lifeboat, the *Solomon Browne*, which was overwhelmed at Tater-du near Lamorna in massive seas on 19 December 1981.

12 Coastal viewpoint

> The question ought not to be 'Are the remains aesthetically pleasing to modern observers?', but 'Did they serve the purpose for which they were designed?'
> Jackson, 1983. *The History & Archaeology of Ports*

The coast holds an eternal dichotomy of the prosaic and the aesthetic. Its length and breadth is filled with functional structures. Many are now indistinct remains or unremarkable buildings but some, like rock lighthouses and tall ships, have so brought to perfection the harmony of form and function that their immediate beauty has made them icons of the maritime past. Such illustrious structures, the work of engineers, have become part of the romance as much as the sea itself, which has long drawn to the coast creative spirits such as artists, photographers and countless writers. For the communities which they observed the coast was a place of intensive labour, from kelp-burning in Orkney, to hauling nets from the Cornish sea. The multifarious tools and workaday buildings, which enabled innumerable families to win their livelihood from the coast, also hold that same beauty which comes from the matching of design and purpose.

The voiceless remains studied by archaeologists can only reveal the practicalities of life in different eras: from the plants and animals eaten in prehistory, to the amount of coal shovelled into the fires of eighteenth-century saltpans. In explaining the age-old connection between the people and the sea, mundane necessity often claims centre stage especially when trying to avoid the bias of current fashionable views. Today a whale cast onto the beach, for instance, is a tragedy of the natural world for which squads of volunteers will rally to the rescue. Place the same event in prehistory and we readily believe that the whale would have been seen as no more than a source of raw materials. Perhaps this is over-simplification. What power would be attributed to the ocean which could cast up such bounty in so monstrous a creature, and which could as easily claim boats and men, and even sweep villages from the dry land?

Similarly, collections of prehistoric artefacts dredged from rivers including the Blyth, Tyne and Wear have been prosaically explained as indicators of ancient crossings or islands, places where objects might be lost. Imagination is needed to seek out the emotional bond between people and the sea, and to propose an alternative view of such objects as ritual deposits of valued possessions. Would the rhythmic tidal waters be any less powerful in the lives and minds of coastal dwellers than water was to people around Flag Fen, near Peterborough? Here Bronze Age trackways and platforms have been linked to the deliberate casting of objects into an inland bay. A focus for such speculation over the beliefs and rituals of coastal dwellers has been provided by the discovery of a timber circle, found in the intertidal area, at Holme-next-the-Sea, Norfolk. Felling dates for the trees suggest that its construction began in the early summer of 2050 BC.

For the coastal communities of more recent centuries, folklore and superstition betray both their distinctness from inland settlements, together with the emotions and beliefs which emanate from their bond with the sea. A few people have been sufficiently bold to set out and walk their country's entire coast but most people know only a small number of coastal haunts. These are often very personal: childhood memories of bays for summer swims and cliff tops for winter walks; holiday destinations in fishing villages or resorts; ferry ports for foreign travel; former or present homes; even, for the lucky few, stretches of coast which have been the focus of their work. Such familiar and favoured locations undoubtedly sing out in the preceding chapters. Against the great sweep of historical knowledge, these personal views of the coast should be valued, for they echo the cognitive-landscapes of past seaboard communities, their mind-held maps of places personally seen or spoken of. Your own familiar stretch of coast is likely to have distinct landward boundaries such as a river or oft-roamed hills and headlands, and more distant features, perhaps an island or promontory whose familiar shape and name you know but have never visited. From prehistory, until roads and railways eased inland travel, this would be the local world of a coastal community, while its wider world would have been constructed from the seamarks, landfalls, havens and trading ports used by its boats and ships. Fresh ideas and skills would have been drawn from within this maritime sphere, and so homes, ornaments, tools, boats and even graves might be quite different from those of neighbouring land communities.

The aesthetic value placed on 'unspoilt' areas of the modern coast has safeguarded archaeological sites ranging from prehistoric burials to post-medieval industries. Back in 1970 the Countryside Commission presented the idea of Heritage Coasts with strict planning controls to protect areas with 'national quality...of scenery and the absence of development for over one or two miles'. Within twenty years an estimated 34% of the coastline was protected and provided with wardens or managers. The Heritage Coasts and other conservation initiatives, especially those facilitating sustainable access to the coast for recreation, have since enabled archaeological sites also to be managed. On sites which might otherwise have suffered degradation, from forces such as agricultural, recreational or natural erosion, it has been possible to undertake investigation and consolidation, and to provide interpretation for the public.

By the late twentieth century many port facilities and waterside industries had become redundant and derelict. In the face of plans for urban renewal, such buildings might survive only if they could accommodate new uses. A lively interest in industrial archaeology, however, spawned champions for the restoration of tide-mills, docks and warehouses, and vessels large and small, while the boom years of the heritage industry provided confidence to initiate preservation projects. Since the growing markets for leisure and recreation featured strongly in plans for regeneration of many old industrial areas, candidates for preservation might win favour beyond their own purist enthusiasts if they contributed to the ambience of the environment and promised to boost visitor numbers.

National agencies responsible for heritage have now developed scoring systems by which to weigh the preservation merits (and funding) of sites as diverse as an Essex decoy pond and a Fife saltworks, or a royal steam yacht and a sewage-sludge dump ship. However, the fate of many historic sites on the coast, as elsewhere, will depend on the

64 The romance of the Tall Ships Race brings thousands to Newcastle's quaysides. The crews of today's vessels upgraded by modern shipping safety regulations, recapture the role of sailors when going aloft was skilled, strenuous and totally essential work regardless of hazards of wind, rain, snow and ice

attitude of local people whose efforts will access resources for their care and interpretation (**colour plate 16**). This book might play a part in setting the wide range of sites from different periods on a level footing where each is understood as a tool in the use of the coast by the communities of the past. In telling their story certain parts of the coast have bustled naturally to the fore. The Channel coast, for example, saw many key events, as proximity to the European mainland made it the contact point for trade or invasion forces travelling to or from these islands. Elsewhere there were hotbeds of activity like the industrial-era ports of the North East, pushed into life by the exploitation of the Great Northern Coalfield, whose maritime communities produced many innovators. Other areas dominate discussion of long past centuries because their local archaeologists have been the first to venture into the mud of rivers, onto the beaches, and beneath the depths of the sea. The examples drawn from these prominent areas, with their museums and heritage attractions, are signposts to other parts of the coast and the history to be found there. For, in so few pages, it was impracticable to cover every coastal activity and innumerate each site, but it has been possible to highlight the breadth of past coastal use and surviving remains. It is for the romance of the coast and the mystique of the past to draw each reader on their own trail of exploration.

In this new century the prospect of coastal change has been pushed to the fore by

65 *While archaeologists and museum curators must submit to budgets and objective policies governing collections and preservation, the public are happily unconstrained and are fondly attached to objects for their sentimental, aesthetic or iconic value*

predictions of global warming. In the tradition of coastal communities there has been vast expenditure on raising defences to hold a status quo between land and sea. There is also the new recognition of the practicality of allowing some areas to be reclaimed by the sea and slowly drowned as tidal wetlands. At the same time the realisation that the sea is now eroding ancient landscapes is drawing archaeologists into the most inaccessible areas of sand dune, marsh, beach and intertidal mud. Here opportunities for preservation in situ for visitors and heritage attractions are improbable. Conditions are uncomfortable, and remains are often difficult to distinguish and under threat of destruction with each incoming wave. Already, archaeologists have found it easier to work by diving at high tide than by struggling with weighty equipment and fragile remains in the short work-time offered at low tide. However, the rewards of study will be great: pollen and plants from submerged peats, hitherto unhoped-for remains of wooden structures and other organic materials, and even the foot and hoofprints of people and animals. This coastal heritage

66 The Neolithic trees lying on this foreshore would have been assumed to be unremarkable casualties of modern coastal erosion had beachwalkers not alerted local archaeologists to the Roman coins which they had found as the shore level began to drop dramatically. (Garry Momber)

should be claimed for present and future generations as much as cliff-top quarries and dock-side cranes. Shipwrecks were once considered remote from the public, limited to visits by small numbers of divers, but remotely operated vehicles and satellite links have enabled seabed expeditions to become mass viewing. Such technology might also deliver the eight-millennia-long story of island Britain as it is rescued from sea-washed sites.

This story of the coast is unending and ever-changing with each tide, storm or cliff-fall. On the countless miles of Britain's coast the living spaces, buildings and tools of preceding generations are continually revealed, re-buried and destroyed; often these windows on the past open and close without anyone to witness them. In this lottery it is the people who live, work and play on the coast, the people who spot the changes, that can raise the alarm which will bring teams of archaeologists to record and salvage.

Further reading

The topics in each chapter have been built up from a miscellany of publications including local guides, port histories and works on industrial archaeological. A few subject specific titles are listed below.

The coast in time and space

Fulford, M., Champion, T. & Long, A. 1997. *England's Coastal Heritage. A Survey for English Heritage and RCHME*. RCHME & English Heritage (Archaeological Report 15).

Animal, vegetable and mineral: extracting resources

Thomson, W. 1983. *Kelp-making in Orkney*. The Orkney Press. Stromness

Yeoman, P. (ed). 1999. *The Salt and Coal Industries at St Monans, Fife in the 18th & 19th Centuries*. Tayside & Fife Archaeological Committee. Monograph Two.

People, goods and ideas: transport

Williams, R.1989. *Limekilns and Limeburning*. Shire Publications Ltd. Princes Risborough.

Martin, N. 1980. *River Ferries*. Terence Dalton, Lavenham.

Platt, R. 1991. *The Ordnance Survey Guide to Smugglers' Britain*. Cassell Publishers Ltd. London.

Defence and control

Saunders, A. 1997. *Book of Channel Defences*. B. T. Batsford/English Heritage, London.

Leisure and health

Lindley, K. 1973. *Seaside Architecture*. Hugh Evelyn. London.

Bainbridge, C. 1986. *Pavilions on the Sea. A History of the Seaside Pleasure Pier.* Robert Hale, London.

Body, G & Eastleigh, R. 1964. *Cliff Railways of the British Isles*. David & Charles. Dawlish.

Havens and markets: creating ports and harbours

Jackson, G. 1983. *The History & Archaeology of Ports and Harbours*. World's Work Ltd. Tadworth

Milne, G. 1985. *The Port of Roman London*. B. T. Batsford, London.

Making and breaking: boat and shipbuilding

Frost, T. 1987. *From Tree to Sea. Building a Wooden Steam Drifter*. Terence Dalton, Lavenham.

Marsden P. 1997. *Ships & Shipwrecks*. B. T. Batsford/English Heritage, London.

Watchers and waiters: regulating the coast

Webb, B.1971. *Coastgaurd! An Official History of the Coastguard*.

Muir, C. 1978. *A Star for Seamen. The Stevenson Family of Engineers*. John Murray Ltd. London

Naish, J. 1985. *Seamarks. Their History and Development*.

Nicholson, C. 1995. *Rock Lighthouses of Britain. The End of An Era?* Whittles Publishing. Latheronwheel.

Lifesaving

Leach, N. 1999. *For Those in Peril. The Lifeboat Service of the United Kingdom and the Republic of Ireland Station by Station*. Silver Link Publishing. Kettering.

Whitaker, B. 1980 *Tynemouth Volunteer Life Brigade*.

A tour of sites

Travelling clockwise around England, Wales and Scotland, this list focuses on places mentioned in the text. Listing does not imply right of access. For sites regularly opened to the public, telephone numbers are quoted as it is advisable to check opening hours and details of current displays. Tourist Information Centres are useful sources on local attractions.

NORTHUMBERLAND
Berwick-upon-Tweed. A walk around the Elizabethan town walls gives views of the river mouth pier (1822) and lighthouse (1826) and leads onto the quayside; across the river is the small Tweed Dock (NT 996524). Ice houses can be seen opposite 25 Ravensbourne. The **Museum & Art Gallery** (Tel. 01289 330933), housed in the old Barracks, includes coble and gear from the salmon fishery, while a small collection in the Town Hall includes objects linked to the town's whaling fleet.

Holy Island is reached via a tidal causeway (NU 080427). The island's historic sites include the castle (NU 136417) dating from 1550 and heavily restored, ruins of an eleventh-century priory (NU 128418) and a bank of lime kilns (1860s).

Bamburgh Castle (NU 183352) rises 150ft (46m) on a rocky outcrop first fortified in the sixth century. Off shore lie the **Farne Islands**, once monastic retreats, and **Longstone Lighthouse** (NU 246389), from whence Grace Darling rowed to the SS *Forfarshire*. The heroine's effigy tops her tomb in Bamburgh graveyard, and the shrine-like **Grace Darling Museum** (NU 178348) is nearby.

Seahouses Harbour (NU 220320). Large collections of traditional fishing gear help the **Marine Life Centre and Fishing Museum** (Tel. 01665 721257) tell the story of the harbour and community. Smoke houses are still at work and the newly built lifeboat house stands to the north of the harbour.

Beadnell harbour and lime kilns (NU 237285). **Beadnell Bay** is typical of Northumberland coast where sand dunes have preserved prehistoric land surfaces and man-made structures but are now threatened by erosion.

Blyth. The port was developed for coal export; its eastern harbour pier now carries a row of wind turbines (NZ 324810). Within the harbour is the Royal Northumberland Yacht Club (NZ 322 805) housed in a nineteenth-century lightship.

Seaton Sluice. There is a small Volunteer Life Brigade Watch House beyond the rock cut (NZ 338768) which enabled ships to enter the tiny river to load coal.

TYNE & WEAR
Cullercoats harbour (NZ 364712) is overlooked by a Volunteer Life Brigade Watch House (1879) and protects the lifeboat house (1896).

Tynemouth. The Priory ruins (NZ 373693) and the modern coastguard station are on a promontory with views of the North Pier. The riverside promenade below the Volunteer Life Brigade Watch House (NZ 372690) overlooks the Black Middens which wrecked SS *Stanley*. **North Shields High Light** (NZ 360683) and **Low Light** (NZ 363684) led ships safely through the river mouth.

Newcastle upon Tyne has both surviving city walls and 1172 castle (Tel. 0191 232 7938). Excavation on the Quayside revealed the medieval riverside. In nearby Broad Chare the museum of

Trinity Maritime Centre (Tel. 0191 261 4691) occupies an eighteenth-century warehouse. At **Dunston** huge coal staithes (NZ 235627) line the river. In Blandford Square **Newcastle Discovery** (Tel. 0191 232 6789) provides a window on selections of Tyne & Wear Museums' extensive maritime collections which range over wooden and metal shipbuilding and technological innovators.

Whickham chuchyard (NZ 209613) contains the grave of Henry Clasper, oarsmen and boatbuilder.

South Shields. The lifeboat *Tyne* (1833) stands in Pier Parade and at the entrance to the South Pier the Volunteer Life Brigade Watch House (1886) overlooks Herd Sands and the octagonal Groyne Light (1883. NZ 369683). On high ground is the extensive fort of **Arbeia** in Baring Street (Tel. 0191 456 1369).

Souter Lighthouse (Tel. 0191 529 3161. NZ 408641), opened in 1871, is complete with keepers cottages.

Sunderland. The Roker Volunteer Life Brigade Watch House (1905. NZ 407594) in Pier View Road overlooks the harbour's North Pier, while the old cast-iron lighthouse (1856. NZ 407598) from the South Pier stands in Cliff Park.

DURHAM AND CLEVELAND
Seaham Harbour (NZ 4349) was built to export coal. Collieries such as Easington (NZ 438442) once tipped spoil over the cliff top.

Hartlepool originally occupied the headland now marked by the Heugh Lighthouse (NZ 534338). The parish church is on the site of seventh-century St Hilda's Abbey. Town walls stand on the south side of the headland and excavations revealed the medieval waterfront. The docks (NZ 514330) have been redeveloped with **Hartlepool Historic Quay** (Tel. 01429 860006), a recreated 1800s waterfront, the **Museum of Hartlepool** (Tel 01429 222255), and historic ships including the **PS *Wingfield Castle***, once a Humber Ferry.

Redcar cares for the world's oldest lifeboat in the **Zetland Lifeboat Museum** (Tel. 01642 494311. NZ 607271). In 1996 erosion of sand at Seaton Carew (NW 296528) briefly revealed the hull of a collier whose remains are now protected by law. Prehistoric peat, forest and man-made structures survive on the beaches around the Tees.

Saltburn-by-the-Sea cliff railway (1884) ascends from the pier head (NZ 666217). The **North Yorkshire and Cleveland Heritage Coast** covers the coastline to Scarborough which was heavily quarried for alum, iron stone and jet.

YORKSHIRE
Staithes village is in the steep valley of a small stream which forms a natural narrow harbour beneath tall cliffs, sheltering the lifeboat house (NZ 784189). The ruinous pier harbour at **Port Mulgrave** (NZ 798177) once sheltered ships carrying iron ore from the cliff.

Whitby has a whale-bone arch on the cliff overlooking the piers which protect the entrance to the harbour whose quaysides follow the River Esk. **Whitby Abbey** (Tel. 01947 603568. NZ 904115) stands on the cliff top opposite. In Pannett Park **Whitby Museum** (Tel. 01947 602908) tells the story of whaling and jet industry. The **Lifeboat Museum** in Pier Road houses the last pulling and sailing lifeboat to be decommissioned: *Robert & Ellen Robinson*.

Ravenscar (NZ 979014). A path from the **National Trust Coastal Centre** (Tel. 01723 870138) leads to **Peak Alum Works** where a waymarked trail has information panels on production from 1650–1850.

Scarborough Castle (Tel. 01723 372451. TA 050893) includes remains of a Roman signal station and tops a promontory whose natural shelter was improved by piers forming a harbour of refuge for eighteenth-century collier fleets. Two cliff railways descend to the South Sands (TA 045880) from the resort town, whose early origins are perpetuated by the Spa (TA 044878).

Filey. The modern lifeboat house (TA 121809) has recreated the 1889 frontage of its predecessor. Erosion of the finger-like promontory **Filey Brigg** (TA 127816) is cutting through a Roman signal station.

Bridlington harbour (TA 185668) was built to shelter colliers. The **National Coastguard Museum** can be visited by appointment (Tel. 01262 606905).

HUMBERSIDE AND LINCOLNSHIRE
The open coast is viciously eroding and the **Spurn Head** lifeboat station (TA 396107) is equipped lest the narrow spit should be breached. The light vessel *Spurn,* once open as a museum, is moored in the marina **Kingston-upon-Hull**. The **Town Docks Museum** (Tel. 01482 613902) in Queen Victoria Square has an extensive whaling display and remains of whalebone arches can be seen at the old museum site in Pickering Park. In Alexander Dock, **Grimsby, The National Fishing Heritage Centre** (Tel. 01472 323345) celebrates the Humber's fishing fleets.

The discovery of Bronze Age boats and the eroding peat on the **North Ferriby** (SE 9825) foreshore highlighted the potential for preservation along the Humber. On the open coast, intertidal remains near **Ingoldmells** (TF 5084) and **Mablethorpe** (TF 5768) related to Iron Age salt making.

Skegness developed as a resort after the railway (1862) linked it to Midlands towns. The A52 leads south east; seaward there are few roads or buildings in reclaimed land, divided by regular drainage ditches and crossed by successive banks of old sea defences.

Boston's 272ft (83m) high church tower, 'the stump', aided navigation five miles inland on the River Witham.

Flag Fen Visitor Centre (Tel. 01733 313414), three miles from Peterborough, displays remarkable finds from peat levels and recreates the Bronze Age landscape.

NORFOLK
King's Lynn is built on land reclaimed from the sea. The **Custom House** (1683) on Perfleet Quay now houses the Tourist Information Centre and an exhibition (Tel. 01553 763044).

The **Norfolk Coast Path** follows a Roman road, the **Peddars Way**, near **Holme-next-the-Sea** from where it may once have continued across the Wash to Lincolnshire. **Brancaster** (TF 7744) is the site of an early third-century Roman fort and harbour in the string of Saxon Shore Forts.

Cromer lifeboat house (TG 220 26) is on the end of the pleasure pier (1901). On this dangerous coast the 110ft (34m) tower of **Happisburg** church probably served as a seamark. It is surrounded by seamen's graves from wrecks of HM Ships *Invincible*, *Peggy* and *Hunter*.

Great Yarmouth has elements of its fourteenth-century town walls. The port combatted the silting and shifting River Yare to maintain its harbour. The railway ensured prosperity as a major fishing port. **Wellington** (1854) and **Britannia** piers (1858, rebuilt 1902) mark its development as a resort. At the head of Breydon water are the bastioned walls of Burgh Castle (TG 474046), another Saxon Shore Fort.

SUFFOLK
Lowestoft. The railway boosted development of both the fishing port and resort town.

Blythburgh church (TM 450753) stands over a tidal estuary which has broken through old marsh embankments. The Blyth enters the sea at **Southwold**, where the lighthouse (TM 509764) is within the holiday town which still sports cannon sent for coastal defence by Charles I.

Dunwich museum (Tel. 01728 648796. TM 475705) and cliff walks explain the dramatic loss of the medieval port. Continuing erosion is an exhibition theme in the **Suffolk Underwater Studies Centre** in Orford. **Snape Maltings** (TM 392574) is on the River Alde at the head of Long Reach around which salt making was an industry. The river no longer enters the sea at **Aldeburgh** where, close to the lifeboat house, the fishing fleet is drawn on to the beach and the position of the **Moot Hall** shows there were once town streets. A Martello tower (TM 462549) guards the landward end of Orford Ness which has pushed the mouths of the Ore and Alde south past **Orford Castle** (Tel. 01394 450472. TM 419499) which showed a light for ships. Martello towers line the coast south from Shingle Street (TM 365425).

Woodbridge tide mill (Tel. 01473 626618. TM 275487) still works close to the town quay. Across the narrow Deben, guided tours are given of the burial where the **Sutton Hoo** ship was found (TM 287486). The broad entrance to the Rivers Orwell and Stour accommodates **The Port of Felixstowe** (TM 2833) which lies opposite **Harwich** where there is a rare treadmill crane (TM 262325).

ESSEX
Colchester lies high on the River Colne, a centre of medieval oyster cultivation. The Norman **Castle Museum** (Tel. 01206 282931) features exhibits from the Roman town. Despite digging an artificial cut the town could not match expanding eighteenth-century ports. Aerial survey, especially around the **Blackwater Estuary,** has revealed numerous decoy ponds, oyster pits and intertidal fish traps. Intertidal survey was pioneered on the **Crouch Estuary**, which leads to Hullbridge, and demonstrated the potential for discovering prehistoric land surfaces.

Maplin Sands lies off a military zone between Foulness Point (TR 048955) and extends into the Thames Estuary. To the west of Shoeburyness is the conurbation of **Southend-on-Sea** with a pier over 2300yd (700m) long (head TR 884849).

Tilbury Fort is England's best and largest example of seventeenth-century military engineering (Tel. 01375 858489. TQ 651754). It was designed to defend the capital.

LONDON
The **Museum of London,** London Wall, (Tel. 020 7600 3699) includes displays on excavated Roman ports. Nineteenth-century **Victoria Dock** (1855. TQ 4080) lies to the east of City Airport. **West India Docks** (1802-6. TQ 37 80) are crossed by the Docklands Light Railway. Near Tower Underground, **St Katharine's Dock** (1835. TQ 339804) now contains a marina and shops in eight acres of docks and warehouses. **London Dock** (1805 TQ 345804), with channels to Shadwell Basin (TQ 352806), can be traced amidst modern buildings. The **Pool of London** with the **Custom House** and **Legal Quay** lay between Tower Bridge and London Bridge.

Sir Joseph Bazalgette's bronze bust is on the Thames Embankment, near Hungerford Bridge. The **Abbey Mills Pumping Station** in Bromley-by-Bow is off Abbey Lane, near the junction with Riverside Road. Nearby on the River Lea, Three Mills Island has the largest surviving tide mill, **House Mill** (1776. Tel. 020 8472 2829), restored with four waterwheels.

Greenwich Observatory (Tel. 020 8312 6557. TQ 389773) is above the Thames in Greenwich Park.

KENT
Chatham Historic Dockyard (Tel. 01634 823800. TQ 758691) is an eighteenth-century dock yard with displays, wreck artefacts and preserved vessels. A viewing gallery gives access to the re-used ships' timbers in the Wheelwright's shop.

The **North Kent Marshes**, which are skirted by the long-distance path the **Saxon Shore Way**, have diverse archaeological potential: **Upchurch** is noted for Roman pottery manufacturing; a Saxon ship was found at **Graveney**; hundreds of eighteenth- and nineteenth-century barges are abandoned in the creeks; and brick and cement making were key industries on the many creeks.

Whitstable Bay was a centre of oyster cultivation and **Whitstable Museum** (Tel. 01227 276998) presents oyster fishing and early wreck salvage diving.

Herne Bay's first pier was destroyed in 1864. Only a short section of its successor (1873) survives, topped by a modern leisure centre (TR 17 684). Neighbouring **Margate** has also lost its pier. **Broadstairs** is on low cliffs around a small bay (TR 398677) where fast ships were built on the sands. In contrast to the resorts, **Ramsgate** developed as a ferry port using a pier harbour built as a refuge for ships driven by rough weather from the **Downs** off Deal. This anchorage and shipwrecks feature in **Ramsgate Maritime Museum** (Tel. 01843 587765. TR 384646), close to the inner or flushing harbour.

Richborough Castle (Tel. 01304 612013. TR 324602) comprises extensive walls of a Roman fort guarding the southern end of the **Wantsum Channel.** This led to the Thames Estuary where twin towers of a ruined church were kept as a Trinity House seamark, and these still mark the remains of a second fort at **Reculver** (TR 227693). The now silted River Stour flows around Richborough to the once flourishing medieval riverfront of **Sandwich** (TR 331582).

Deal has a modern pleasure pier of steel and reinforced concrete (1957. TR 378526). From 1853 the **Time Ball Tower** (Tel. 01304 201200) on the sea front signalled 12.00 noon to ships in the Downs. Nearby fishing boats are drawn onto the steep beach in front of the intact Henry VIII **Deal Castle** (Tel. 01304 372762. TR 377521). The contemporary **Walmer Castle** (Tel. 01304 364288. TR 377500) was converted to a dwelling for the Lord Warden of the Cinque Ports. **Walmer lifeboat house** (TR 377515) has been extended without altering its character.

Dover Castle (Tel. 01304 201628) is extensive and well-preserved. It includes the **Roman lighthouse** (TR 325418) and nineteenth-century tunnels within the cliff used for co-ordinating the Dunkirk evacuation. There are extensive fortifications on the **Western Heights** (TR 310405), first built in 1779 and improved in 1803–15 and the 1860s. Spiral stairs in the **Grand Shaft** led to the town. There are cliff-top viewpoints (TR 335422) for **Admiralty Harbour** and the **Langdon Bay** Bronze Age wreck site (TR 341417). **Dover Museum** (Tel. 01304 201066), in Market Square, displays bronzes from the Langdon Bay Wreck, the Bronze Age boat found beneath the underpass for the A20, and models which show the development of the harbour, .

Folkestone developed as both packet port and resort. The cliff railway still operates. Martello towers stretch from here to Seaford; **Dymchurch tower** is open to the public (Tel. 01304 211067. TR 102294). From Hythe the **Royal Military Canal** (TR 188349) forms a boundary to Romney Marsh and Dungeness. Remains of **Lympne's** Roman fort and port (TR 117342) lie inland of the canal.

EAST AND WEST SUSSEX
Rye is on high ground with a medieval gatehouse at its entrance. Coastal change trapped a ship in the bed of the old Rother and ships' timbers in gravels at Camber, and left Henry VIII's **Camber Castle** (Tel. 01797 223862. TQ 921184) inland. Fishing boats lie below the town and dredgers visit the aggregate wharf downstream. The lifeboat house (TQ 943 190) is in **Rye Harbour**, where there is a Martello tower (TQ 941188), while the old lifeboat house (TQ 931178) lies to the west. Peat beds uncover off **Pett Level** (TQ 9014).

Hastings resort seafront stretches east from the pier (1917. TQ 812088) towards the hill-top castle ruins (Tel. 01424 781111. TQ 820094). From Rock-a-Nore Road a cliff railway rises above the **Shipwreck Heritage Centre** (Tel.01424 437452. TQ 828094) that houses a Rother Barge, remains of a Roman ship from London, and huge medieval rudders trawled from the bay. On the beach close by are the **Fishermen's Museum** (formerly a fishermen's chapel, Tel. 01424 461446) and netshops, and the fishing fleet draws up before the lifeboat house.

Beyond **Bexhill** the low coast is guarded by Martello towers. **Pevensey Castle** (Tel. 01323 762604. TQ 645048) includes remains of a Saxon Shore Fort and carries 1939–45 defences.

Beachy Head Lighthouse (TV 583950) is 142ft (43m) tall and can be viewed from the 534ft-high

(163m) cliffs. The **Belle Tout Lighthouse** has been moved back from its cliff-edge site (TV563954).

Newhaven formed after a storm shifted the mouth of the River Ouse. Its role as a ferry port was promoted by the railway. The cliff path leads west to the planned town of **Peacehaven** (TQ 3900 – TQ 4200).

Brighton Marina (TQ 340030) with its floating inshore rescue boathouse lies below high chalk cliffs at the eastern end of the town. From here the modern **Volks Railway** runs parallel with the two-tier promenade to the **Palace Pier** (TQ 313037), beyond which is the truncated and derelict West Pier. The original fishing village lay in front of the Steyne where the **Royal Pavilion** stands. The quieter resort of **Hove** lies to the west.

Shoreham (TQ 208060) was supplanted by **Shoreham-by-Sea** as the mouth of the River Adur migrated. A power station (TQ 247048) was a landmark of the new port's harbour which lies parallel to the coast.

Bognor is a planted Victorian resort which took the name Bognor Regis after George V recuperated in the town. The already shortened pier (SZ 938987) of 1865 was further damaged by storms in 1999.

Chichester Harbour is a natural inlet whose historic importance is apparent from **Fishbourne Roman Palace** (Tel. 01243 785859. SU 839048) which lies close to its upper reaches.

HAMPSHIRE
Hayling Island, victim of ancient and modern erosion, divides **Chichester** and **Langstone Harbours**. Extensive survey, including underwater excavation of timber structures, has mapped the archaeological resource of Langstone from Bronze Age burials and flint-working to eighteenth-century salterns.

Portsmouth Harbour was defended as a naval base. **Portchester Castle** (Tel. 023 92378291. SU 625046) has the highest surviving walls of Saxon Shore Forts. Henry VIII's **Southsea Castle** (Tel. SZ 643980), topped by a lighthouse since 1823, guards the seaward approaches. In the mid-nineteenth century the defensive ring was extended with Solent forts including **Spit Bank** (SZ 636971) and **Horse Sand** (SZ 655949), and forts along Portsdown Hill including **Fort Nelson** (Tel. 01329 233734. SU 607 072) which houses part of the Royal Armouries collection. A ferry (SU 628000) links Portsmouth with Gosport, home of **Haslar Naval Hospital** (SZ 618988). The sewage of Victorian Portsmouth was pumped to sea by **Eastney Beam Engine House** (Tel. 023 92827261) in Henderson Road, and modern outfalls discharged close to the protected wreck **HMS Invincible** (lost 1758. SZ 679937). **Portsmouth Historic Dockyard** (Tel. 023 92861533) includes the *Mary Rose* while the harbour now shelters a continental ferry port and marinas including **Haslar** and **Port Solent** (SU 6305).

Southampton Water laps the country park (Tel. 01703 455157) at Netley where only the chapel and cemetery survive from the **Royal Victoria Hospital** (SU 464073). **Southampton's** Saxon port lay on the Itchen. Replacing the ferry, **Itchen Bridge** (SU 433382) now gives views of the aggregate wharfs. The ruined castle belonged to the Norman port on the Test. There are walks around the extensive walls (Tel. 023 80221160) where God's Tower houses the **Museum of Archaeology** (Tel. 023 80635904) which explains city excavations. On Town Quay the medieval **Wool House** is the Maritime Museum (Tel. 023 80223941). The Victorian docks have been redeveloped to include **Ocean Village** (SU 429109) where the sewage dump ship **SS *Shieldhall*** berths (Tel. 023 80225853). The Union Castle offices opposite Canute Place betray the work of an international packet port. Local ferries ply to **Hythe Pier** (SU 427085). The lifeboat *Arthur & Ruby Read* is preserved in **Hythe Marina** (SU 4208). In a backwater of the Test, **Eling Tide Mill** (Tel. 023 80869575. SU 365125) still grinds corn. **Fawley Oil Refinery** covers a huge area (centred SU 450040) and the power station can be seen from Henry VIII's **Calshot Castle** (Tel. 023 80892023. SU 488 024) where an activity centre occupies the site of a **Royal Naval Flying Station**.

Lepe Foreshore Country Park (SZ 455985) includes a caisson construction site for the Normandy landings. Coastguard cottages (SZ 450985) overlook the entrance to Beaulieu River. **Bucklers Hard Museum** (Tel. 01590 616203. SU 408000) interprets the surviving eighteenth-century shipbuilding village.

The **Solent Way** from **Lymington** to **Keyhaven** passes marshes where salt making was intensive. It follows the shingle spit to Henry VIII's **Hurst Castle** (Tel. 01590 642344. SZ 317897) which has mid-nineteenth-century armoured casemates.

ISLE OF WIGHT
Ferries to **West Cowes** pass the **Royal Yacht Squadron,** one of twin Henry VIII forts which stood at the mouth of the Medina. The river divides the Island, whose centre is guarded by **Carisbrooke Castle** (Tel. 01983 522107. SZ 486874). The site of **East Medina Mills** tide pond is now a marina (SZ 510920). Queen Victoria's residence **Osborne House** (Tel. 01983 200022. SZ 516831), home of the royal bathing machine, lies above East Cowes.

Fishbourne Beach, the site of survey and excavation of prehistoric land surfaces and structures, is partially owned by **Quarr Abbey** (SZ 562927). **Ryde Pier** (SZ 593937) was opened in 1813; in 1880 it was widened and a railway added which is still the landing point for ferries.

Culver Down is topped by defences and gives views east to the **Nab Tower** and south-west to the resort towns where **Sandown Pier** survives (SZ 598839*).* **Ventnor's** promenade rises to low cliff walks which eventually reach the undercliff and **St Catherine's Lighthouse** (SZ 497753). The fourteenth-century **lighthouse** (SZ 494773) on St Catherines Hill, above **Blackgang Chine,** looks along a notorious shipwreck coast to coastguard cottages at **Atherfield (**SZ 452793)

Palmerston's **Needles Battery** (Tel. 01983 754772. SZ 295849) is reached from **Alum Bay** where a chairlift (SZ 307 855) descends close to the site of the old pier. Piers survive at **Totland** (SZ 322871) and next to Henry VIII's **Yarmouth Castle** (Tel. 01983 760678. SZ 354898). There is a pillbox on **Freshwater causeway** (SZ 347872).

DORSET
Christchurch Harbour (SZ 1791) would have provided natural shelter for Iron Age ships unloading goods for the settlement on **Hengistbury Head** (SZ 1790*).* Views west show the massive post-railway expansion of the previously exclusive **Bournemouth** which still operates three cliff railways.

Poole Bay has seen the discovery of classical Mediterranean-style stone anchors. **Poole Harbour** has been a focus for human activity in all periods. **Poole Waterfront Museum** (Tel. 01202 683138. SZ 008903) occupies the medieval quayside buildings close to the Custom House. At the head of the harbour is **Wareham** (SZ 9288) with its originally Saxon walls.

Swanage quayside still carries rails used for transporting stone to waiting ships. Town trails include the pier, lifeboat house and old preventative station. Boat trips visit the quarried cliffs which can be viewed from **Durlston Head** (SZ 035772) where there is a stone globe.

St Aldhelm's Chapel (SY 960755), a twelfth-century light, is reached by foot on a track leading to the cliff-top **Coastguard Houses** (SY 960756). To the west are the cliffs of **Kimmeridge** (SY 9078) which were mined for shale. Neighbouring **Wolbarrow Bay** was the fishing ground for villagers from **Tyneham** (Tel. 01929 462721, ext. 4819. SY 895816) whose ruins and schoolhouse displays are open when firing range use permits.

Weymouth Time Walk (Tel. 01305 777622) in Brewer's Quay presents the resort's past including a bathing machine reputedly used by George III. Occupied since at least the Mesolithic, the **Isle of Portland** has a lighthouse (Tel. 01305 861233) at its tip. Henry VIII's **Portland Castle** (Tel. 01305 820539. SY 684743), built of local stone from the extensive quarries, overlooks the massive harbour whose breakwaters were constructed from quarry waste.

Lyme Regis provided a medieval haven by building a stone breakwater, the Cobb, which is now walked on as a pleasure pier.

DEVON AND CORNWALL
Exeter has fragments of its Roman walls. The **Custom House** is on the quayside where warehouses have been re-used alongside modern buildings. The canal was cut in 1563 to reach **Topsham** where shipbuilding docks are preserved in the shape of underground car parks for flats built above.

Babbacombe cliff railway still operates (SX 926658) in **Torquay. Kent's Cavern** (Tel. 01803 215136. SX 935642), which contained palaeolithic remains, is in **Torquay.** Nearby, a protected wreck site off **Moor Sand** (SX 759361) saw recovery of swords, part of a Bronze Age boat's cargo. Another protected site in the **Erme Estuary** (SX 606466) preserved tin ingots, the cargo of a Roman period or earlier wreck.

Plymouth Sound is a natural inlet sheltered by a man-made and fortified breakwater. On Plymouth Hoe is Smeaton's 1759 **Eddystone Lighthouse** (Tel. 01752 600608). There are guided tours of the nearby **Royal Citadel** (Tel. 01752 775841) constructed in 1665, and of the 1830s **Royal William Yard** (Tel, 01752 775841) which victualled the fleet. The Naval Base was defended by a ring of batteries and forts including **Fort Bovisand** (SX 487506), now an underwater centre, and **Crownhill Fort** (Tel. 01752 793754. SX 487592). Walks leaflets introduce others such as **Bowden Battery,** now a garden centre.

Cawsand Bay (SX 4350) was an anchorage before Plymouth breakwater was built. Pilchard cellars are recorded here in the sixteenth century. **Eddystone Lighthouse** lies some 9 miles off Rame Head.

Par harbour (SX 0753) silted with china clay. At **Charlestown Shipwreck Heritage Centre** (Tel. 01762 69897. SX 038517) visitors follow the route of china clay through tunnels to the preserved harbour where it was loaded into ships. **Pentewan** (SX 0147) harbour was also built for china clay export.

The Dodman (SX 002395) is the south-west's largest cliff castle. Inside are two Bronze burial mounds, a medieval strip field system and an early nineteenth-century watch house. The site of an Iron Age cliff castle was chosen for Henry VIII's **Pendennis Castle** (Tel. 01326 316594. SW 824318) which fortifies the eastern headland of the Fal Estuary. **Cadgwith** (SW 721145) is an old pilchard fishing village, where the pilchard cellar is now a restaurant.

Porthleven harbour (SW 628257) was built speculatively (1811–23) as a harbour of refuge. The old lifeboat house stands at its entrance (SW 625255). The fishing harbour of **Penzance** (SW 476302) had piers rebuilt in the mid-eighteenth century.

Penlee Lifeboat Station (SW 473270) is north of **Mousehole** which has a pier harbour (SW 469263). **Tater-du Lighthouse** (1968. SW 440230) is beyond **Lamorna** (SW 4523), a natural cove where granite was loaded. **Treryn Dinas** is a large cliff castle (SW 397221).

Longships Lighthouse (SW 109252) stands to westwards of Land's End and **Wolf Rock Lighthouse** (SW 268119) lies 9 miles (15km) to the south-west. **Bishop Rock Lighthouse** (SV 807064) marks the western edge of the **Isles of Scilly**; in fine weather there are boat trips from **Hugh Town** on St Mary's. Here walks lead around the **Garrison Walls** (SV 898104) , which fortify the headland, to **Star Castle** (1593). Prehistoric field boundaries on **Samson** spread into the intertidal area on Samson Flats (SV 880128). A good example of a stone lined kelp pit is at **Tinkler's Hill** (SX 916 165).

St Ives (SW 5140) prospered in the pilchard fishery and supported the mining industry. Smeaton built its quay in 1767. Near St Agnes the South West Coast Path to **Cligga Head** (SW 737537) passes workings and cliffs stained by waste water from tin and copper mines.

Tintagel (SX 050892). Excavation showed that this spectacular rock was a sixth-century Royal seat. Remains include ruins of a dramatically located thirteenth-century castle (Tel. 01840 770328).

Westward Ho! was founded in 1863 and the resort boasted England's first golf course. **Lynton** is linked to **Lynmouth** by the cliff railway, built in 1890.

SOMERSET, AVON AND GLOUCESTERSHIRE
Somerset Levels Peat Centre (Tel. 01458 860697. ST 425414), Westhay near Glastonbury, displays objects excavated from the peats and explains prehistoric occupation of wetlands.

Steep Holm (ST 22 and 2360) is an island in the Bristol Channel chosen for a Roman signal station.

Weston-Super-Mare. The 1040ft pleasure pier (1867) crosses the sand to **Birnbeck Island** where there is a lifeboat station (ST 305625). **Clevedon Pier** (1975. ST 401719) has been restored after a 200ft section collapsed.

Avonmouth Docks (entrance lock ST 506788) saved large vessels negotiating the narrow winding river to **Bristol** where preservation of the **SS *Great Britain*** (Tel.0117 9291843) celebrates the port's role in transatlantic travel. She lies in a dry dock (ST 576722) off the 1803 **Floating Harbour** whose work is kept alive by the **Bristol Industrial Museum** (Tel. 0117 9251470).

Gloucester Docks provided a transhipment point for inland navigation. Housed in a warehouse the **National Waterways Museum** (Tel. 01452 318054) includes a display on spoon dredgers.

The **Wild Fowl and Wetland Trust** (Tel. 01453 890333) in Slimbridge has a working nineteenth-century decoy pond now used for bird studies.

GWENT AND GLAMORGAN
The **Severn Bridge** (service station viewpoint ST 568899) has a main span of 3240ft. The **Second Severn Crossing** prompted an archaeological survey which has examined prehistoric land surfaces and structures in the intertidal area off the **Caldicot Levels**. **Chepstow Castle** stands over the navigable River Wye. **Newport Castle** (ST 313883) is similarly by the River Usk where a dock was opened in 1842, and a power station is now at its mouth (ST 32 83); its antiquity is indicated by **Caerleon** Roman fort and ampitheatre (Tel. 01633 422518. ST 338903). Downstream the **Wentlooge Levels** (centred ST 270810) retain a Roman drainage pattern which extends beyond the later sea defences.

Cardiff Castle (Tel. 029 20878100) reused a Roman fortified site. After opening its first dock in 1839 the city rose to export half the output of South Wales coalfields. The **Welsh Industrial and Maritime Museum** (Tel. 029 20497039) is in Bute Street, the dock area. Across the estuary mouth, **Penarth** exported coal and also developed as a resort. In 1880 **Barry Island** (ST 1166) was joined to the mainland to form coal exporting docks which prompted explosive expansion.

Kenfig Burrows (centred SS 790820). The sands have covered a twelfth-century settlement.

Port Talbot created docks to export copper and a steelworks supported construction of its new harbour (centred SS 748878). **Swansea**, like Bristol, created floating harbours from its river and developed as a general cargo port.

DYFED
Kidwelly Castle (Tel. 01554 890104. SN 409071), standing at the tidal limit of the River Gwendraeth, is extensive and well preserved.

There are extensive intertidal peat beds off **Ferryside,** and drowned forest on **Marros Sands** (SN 206074) and at the east end of **Amroth** (SN 163070) beach. From the cliffs to the west iron ore was shipped off the beaches. **Saundersfoot** harbour (SN 137046) was built to export coal.

Tenby's ruined castle (SN 137004) is on a promontory shared by the current lifeboat house. The harbour below dries but there is a sluicing dock. Old lifeboat houses can be seen in the corner of the harbour and on Castle sands. There is a stone fish-trap (SS 122986), best seen from **Giltar Point** (SS 123984) where limestone was once quarried and loaded into ships.

Milford Haven is an extensive waterway accommodating tankers berthing at oil refineries. The **River Pembroke** gives its name to town, Norman castle (Tel. 01646 684585. SM 981013) and nineteenth-century naval dockyard (SM 9503). **Milford Haven Museum** (Tel. 01646 694496), in the town's docks, is housed in a store built in 1797 for whale oil. It covers the port's two ages of oil, whale and crude. **Carew** has Wales's only restored tide-mill (Tel. 01646 651782. SN 041037).

Solva is a narrow inlet with a bank of limekilns (SM 808421). Its quay was built in 1861 to handle stone for the **Smalls Lighthouse** (SM 466088), 15 miles (27km) off St David's.

Aberaeron is a planned nineteenth-century town. Its harbour (SN 456628) exported agricultural produce and strongly built wooden schooners. The university town of **Aberystwyth** is a resort with pier (1865 since reduced) and cliff railway (SN 586825) but also has harbour piers (SN 579809) at the mouth of the Rheidol.

GWYNEDD
Porthmadog Maritime Museum (Tel. 01766 513736. SH 569384) occupies an old slate shed on Oakley Wharf and tells of the port's expansion based on schooners exporting slate worldwide. Trails show the land formed from discharged ballast.

Caernarfon Castle (Tel. 01286 677617. SH 478622) is at the south-west end of the Menia Strait. It stands on the riverfront of a walled town originally fortified by the Romans. The **Menai Bridge** (SH 557713) leads to Anglesey where **Beaumaris Castle** (Tel. 01248 810361. SH 607762) guards the Strait's north-east end. At the eastern tip is **Trwyn Du Lighthouse** (SH 641815). The exposed location has attracted a wind farm, while the isolated coast at **Y Borthwen** has ruins of a brickworks (SH 402946). *Mary* (SH 265 47), a protected wreck site, is close to the **Skerries Lighthouse** (SH 267 947).

Llandudno is a resort with two seafronts, and a lifeboat station (SH 779821) between the two. The town lies beneath the promontory of the **Great Orme** on which a **Bronze Age Copper Mine** (Tel. 01492 870447) has been excavated.

CLWYD, CHESHIRE, MERSEYSIDE AND LANCASHIRE
Inland from **Rhyl** harbour the River Clwyd was deepened for ships to reach **Rhuddlan Castle** (Tel. 01745 590777). **Chester** (SJ 4065) was a Roman port but medieval silting of the Dee ended that role for the walled city and later left **Neston** (SJ 2977) and **Parkgate** (SJ 278781) fronted by marsh rather than water.

New Brighton seafront, which has lost both its pleasure pier and tower, runs to the mouth of the Mersey, guarded by **Perch Rock Battery** (1829). Across the river, wind turbines turn on **Seaforth** waterfront. Ships on the Mersey relied on time signals from **Bidston Hill** now topped by an Observatory. The **Wallasey Ferry** crosses to the redeveloped docks. The rise of Liverpool through the slave trade is explained in **Merseyside Maritime Museum** (Tel. 0151 207 0001), in one warehouse of **Albert Dock** which also includes the **HM Customs & Excise National Museum**.

The resort towns of **Southport, Lytham St Annes, Blackpool** and **Cleveleys** line 15 miles of coast. They flourished after the railway linked them with inland Lancashire. **Fleetwood** prospered as both resort and major fishing port.

Lancaster is a Roman town with a Norman castle. Along the River Lune St Georges Quay includes the old Custom House, a **Maritime Museum** (Tel. 01524 64637). After silting, docks were built at downriver **Glasson** (SD 446559).

CUMBRIA AND DUMFRIES & GALLOWAY

Laying rails around the sinking sands of **Morecombe Bay** assisted technological advance in pier building. On its western edge **Barrow-in-Furness** shipbuilding advanced through nineteenth-century exploitation of local iron ore. The docks' entrance (SD199672) is sheltered by the long Isle of Walney. **Furness Abbey** (Tel. 01229 823420. SD 218717) and the island ruins of fourteenth-century **Piel Castle** (SD 233636) betray the earlier use of the waterway.

Ravenglass Roman fort is at the mouth of the River Esk. It has little visible remains save the well preserved bathhouse (NY 088961).

St Bees Lighthouse (NX 941143) is some 400ft (122m) above the sea. The village grew around a seventh-century priory.

Whitehaven is considered the most complex of pier harbours (centred NX 975185) since this major coal exporter underwent successive improvements during the eighteenth and nineteenth centuries. **Workington** saw less harbour development due to rivalry between coal owners. Its single dock (NX 991 294) was opened in 1856. **Maryport Maritime Museum** (Tel. 01900 813738) in Senhouse Street is close to the port's two docks (centred NY 031366), now redeveloped, which supplemented river coal staithes. **Senhouse Roman Museum** (Tel. 01900 816168) reveals the town as the site of a fort in the chain south from Hadrian's Wall. **Bowness-on-Solway** marks the Wall's end.

Mote of Mark (NX 845540) is an Iron Age fort on Rough Firth. The **Isle of Whithorn** still has a St Ninian's chapel (NX 479364); the early monastery was a centre for foreign imports.

STRATHCLYDE

Ayr, with harbour and riverside quays (NS 3322), is an ancient port and major resort, and a nearby holiday camp opened an early chairlift (NS 301180). **Irvine** is home to the **Scottish Maritime Museum** (Tel. 01294 278283) which has full-size vessels and presents Scottish shipbuilding. The promontory at **Troon** (NS 312 311) shelters docks while the surrounding golf courses make it St Andrews of the west. **Ardrossan** harbour (NS 225422), served by the railway, shelters ferries for the **Isle of Arran**, where prehistoric activity included quarrying stone for axes. The islands raised beaches show changes in land and sea level.

Cloch Point Lighthouse (1791. NS 202758) overlooks the mouth of the Clyde. The impressive **Greenock Custom House** (NS 282763), housing the **Custom & Excise Museum** (Tel. 01457 726331), indicates the port's nineteenth-century success over upstream **Glasgow**. Neighbouring docks eastwards to **Port Glasgow** are the East India Harbour, Victoria Dock and James Watt Dock; the container terminal (NS 279768) is to the west. River trips down the Clyde pass lighted buoys marking the remains of shoals and demolished training walls. Shipbuilding yards continue the tradition of metal shipbuilding made possible by dredging the river. Clyde paddlesteamers carried Lanarkshire workers to growing resorts including **Helensburgh,** and **Rothesay** on the Isle of Bute where there are ruins of a circular thirteenth-century castle (NS 087645).

HIGHLAND AND WESTERN ISLES

Construction in stone left the many prehistoric structures of northern Scotland more durable and visible than their southern counterparts. While their remoteness from present-day urban centres of population contributes to their survival, it has also meant fewer occurences to prompt discovery, study and curation. Specific archaeological surveys, for example on the Outher Hebridean island of **Barra**, have traced the landscape to which monuments belong and demonstrated the range and intensity of prehistoric activity. Threats include sand blow outs, quarrying and afforestation.

By **Glen Elg Bay** are the ruins of Bernera Barracks (NG 815197), built in 1722 to support military control of the Highlands. Nearby, in **Gleann Beag**, a tall ruined broch has galleried walls (NG 829172). To the north a ferry (NG 794214) runs on the old cattle crossing to **Kylerhea**, Isle of Skye, from which the main ferry route is now bridged to **Kyle of Lochalsh** (NG 760271) with its rail terminal. **Eilean Donan Castle** (NG 881258) occupies an islet where Loch Alsh is formed from

Lochs Duich and Long.

Ullapool was established in 1788 as a herring station but has prospered as a resort and ferry port with sailings from the pier (NH 128948) across Loch Broom and for Stornaway, Lewis. **Kinlochbervie**'s natural harbour (NC 221561) with protective pier provided shelter for a modern deep-sea fishing fleet.

Cape Wrath Lighthouse (NC 257747), built in 1827, demonstrates the logistical problems of lighthouse construction and supply. It is an 11-mile minibus journey to 900 ft high cliffs from the **Keodale** ferry across the **Kyle of Durness**. **Loch Eriboll**, a naval anchorage, has a bank of lime kilns (NC 446596) surrounded by quarries. Flagstones were the export of nineteenth-century **Thurso**, ferry port for the Orkney. Flagstone production is explained at **Castleton** in the preserved quarry (ND 193084) and small, stone-piered harbour (ND 197086).

Wick was a harbour for herring fleets. South and inland lie the three near-complete burial monuments; the **Grey Cairns of Camster** (ND 260440). A small pier in a natural cove formed the harbour for **Latheronwheel** (ND 191322) a mile inland. At **Badbea** (ND 088201) a monument marks the steep site of a cliff-top village to which crofters were relocated by land clearances.

ORKNEY
The islands have a high density of well preserved prehistoric monuments. These include settlements on Mainland at **Skara Brae** (Tel. 01856 841815. HY 229187) and Papa Westray at **Knap of Howar** (HY 483518). Also on Mainland, the **Stones of Stenness** (HY 307125) and the **Ring of Brogar** (HY 294133) are dramatically sited at the junction between two lochs with the remarkable tomb of **Maes Howe** close by (HY 318127. Access via Tormiston Mill Tel. 01856 761606). A Pictich/Viking settlement has been excavated at **Buckquoy** (HY 242283). The Viking waterfront of **Kirkwall** is beneath the later town which has Britain's most northerly cathedral, twelfth-century St Magnus. **Tankerness House Museum** in Broad Street (Tel. 01856 873191) displays a few items from the kelp burning industry. The best remains of the industry are on Sanday including pits (HY 679459). **Stromness** was a crewing port for whaling ships and its local trails include significant buildings along the historic waterfront and main street. World War I and II fleets used **Scapa Flow** which was made secure by **Churchill Barriers** between Mainland and Burray. Oil is brought ashore to Orkney and **Burgar Hill** (HY 343262) is the site of alternative power generation using wind turbines.

SHETLAND
The islands have a high density of well preserved prehistoric monuments. Neolithic/Bronze Age settlements include the **Scoud of Brouster** (HU 255516) with walls and fields, and two houses at **Ness of Gruting** (HU 276483). Boat trips reach the best-preserved broch in Scotland, **Mousa** (HU 456237), which is over 13m tall. At **Underhoull** on Unst is a broch and excavated early Norse houses (HP 573044). The sea-eroded site of **Jarlshoff**, Sumburgh, (HU 399096) has a visitor centre interpreting 3,000 years of occupation (Tel. 01595 460112).

The **Kennermerland** is a protected wreck on the Out Skerries (HU 688 713) on which seventeenth-century golf clubs were found.

GRAMPIAN AND TAYSIDE
Burghead comprises a nineteenth-century town and harbour sheltered by the promontory whose tip was a Pictish fort (NJ 108691). **Cullykhan** promontory fort (NJ 838664) lies by a small bay.

On the eastern side of the Spey's mouth, **Tugnet Ice House** (Tel. 01309 673701. NJ 348654), reputely Scotland's largest industrial icehouse, is seasonally opened as a museum of the local salmon station. **Buckie's** large harbour (NJ 430 660) was built in 1870s, and **Buckie Drifter** (Tel. 01542 834646) portrays the local herring fishing industry. **Portsoy** built its harbour (NJ 589663) in the seventeenth century and exported serpentine.

Scotland's Lighthouse Museum (Tel. 01346 511022) includes the first Kinnaird Head lighthouse which in 1787 was added to a castle overlooking **Fraserburgh's** originally sixteenth-century harbour.

Rattray (NK 087578) was a port until a storm left the Loch of Strathbeg landlocked.

Peterhead sent whaling ships to the Arctic and then rose with herring fishing. In addition to the docks (NK 137 62) the bay has protective piers which were built by convicts between 1886 and 1958. **Aberdeen** had a whaling fleet and successful shipbuilders. **Aberdeen Maritime Museum** in Shiprow is near the quays. The road to **Girdleness Lighthouse** (NJ 971053) gives views of the port, which now supports the oil and gas industry, and river mouth piers.

Dunottar Castle (Tel. 01569 762173. NO 881939) occupies a 160ft-high crag south of **Stonehaven**.

Montrose lies at the mouth of a natural harbour. The **Museum & Art Gallery** (Tel. 01674 673232) includes a display on whaling and sealing.

Arbroath has a compact pier harbour (NO 643405). The **Signal Tower** (Tel. 01241 875598) in Ladyloan houses displays on the construction of the **Bell Rock Lighthouse**, whose keepers it accommodated, and on local fishing and smoking.

Broughty Castle (Tel. 01382 436916. NO 464304), originally sixteenth-century, guards the entrance to the Firth of Tay. Its exhibits include a whaling gallery. From the 1830s **Dundee** boomed on imported jute. Victoria Dock, under redevelopment, now shelters the 1824 **HMS *Unicorn*** (Tel. 01382 200900) and the **North Carr Light Vessel**.

FIFE, LOTHIAN AND BORDERS

St Andrews, famed for its historic golf course, has a ruined Norman castle (Tel. 01334 477196), cathedral and small harbour. Beside **Anstruther** harbour, historic quayside buildings house the **Scottish Fisheries Museum** (Tel 01333 310628).

St Monans Salt Works (NO 533018) has been excavated and landscaped with information boards. The wind engine tower provides a viewing platform in the summer.

The **Isle of May**'s lighthouse (NT 654993) was first built in the seventeenth century.

Queensferry harbour (NT 120788) received royal patronage in the twelfth century to assist pilgrims en route to St Andrews. The ferries' work ended with the **Forth Road Bridge** (NT 124780), Britain's longest when opened in 1964 with a 3300ft main span. The **Forth Rail Bridge** (NT 127784), with the longest span in the world on completion in 1890, replaced the world's first rail ferry which used **Burntisland** docks (NT 233854). To the east, **Cramond** (NT 1876) was the site of a Roman supply base.

Edinburgh's waterfront has three ports with pier harbours. **Granton** (NT 2377), whose piers sheltered steam colliers, has been partially infilled. **Newhaven Heritage Centre** (Tel. 0131 551 4165) is in the redeveloped fishmarket beside the small fishing harbour (NT 254772). **Leith** (NT 2677 to NT 27 26) is a huge complex of docks beyond the river port which is upstream of the old Custom House (NT 270769). There is a Martello tower (NT 269777) on the broad outer arm of the harbour.

Traprain Law (NT 580748) is a distinctive hill fortified in the Iron Age. **Dunbar's** ruined castle is at the mouth of the pier-enclosed fishing harbour (NT 679793) of this old whaling port.

St Abbs Lighthouse (NT 914692) is on high cliffs and has no tower. The fishing port of **Eyemouth** has a long narrow harbour (NT 946643) within the river.

Index

Ice and Icehouses 40, 64-5, 142, 153
Ingoldmells 19, 144
Ipswich 22
Iron 44, 57, 90, 150, pl.12; plating 77, 79, 102, 105, 109; lighthouses 122, 143; shipbuilding 113
Isle of May 67, 154
Isles of Scilly 19, 24, 25, 30, 43, 77

Jarlshoff 21, 153

Kelp and Kelp burning 43-4, 136, 149, 153
Kenfig 30
Kent's Cavern 12, 35, 149
Keyhaven 50, 146
Kidwelly Castle 53, 150
Kimmeridge 46, 148
King's Lynn 116, 144
Kinlochbervie 40, 153
Kirkwall 21, 27, 44, 153
Knap of Howar 15, 153
Kylerhea 68, 152

Lamorna 46, 135, 149
Lancaster 116, 151
Land's End 60, 62
Langdon Bay 60, 146
Langstone Harbour 55, 147
Latheronwheel **100**, 153
Leather 45
Legal Quays 116
Leisure 32, 81-95
Leith 42, 53, 55, 82, **111**, 119, 154
Lepe 95, **118**, 148
Liddell, Richard 57
Lifeboat 95, 118, 126, 129-135; **131**, **132**; houses 126, 129-135, **134, 135**, 143, 144, 145, 146, 148, 149, 150, 151; Service board **134**, 135
Lifesaving 33-4, 118, 126-135
Lighthouses 23, 27, 46,125, 136, 143, 144, 148, 151, 152, 153; development 119-123; leading lights **121**, 142; lanterns 123-4; Bell Rock 122, 154; Belle Tout 27, 147; Bishop Rock 46, 149; Dungeness 123; Eddystone 122, 125, 149; Girdleness pl.15; Longships 46, 149; Longstone 142; St Abbs pl.15; St Bees 123, 152; St Catetherine's 120; Smalls 123, 151; South Foreland 123; Souter 122, **123**, 143; Tater-du 135, 149; Wolf Rock 46, 149
Light vessels 85, **86**, 142, 144
Lime and Limestone 46, 54, 60, 65-6, 143, 150, 151, 153, pl.6, 7
Liverpool 96, 101, 102, 117, 130, 151, pl.12
Llandudno 132, 151
Llanelli 102

Loch Eriboll 66, 153, pl.6, 7
London 22, 27, 42, 46, 55, 56, 65, 67, 70, 80, 85, 88, 90, 113, 125, 129; docks 102, **103**, 145; port of 101, **99**; Roman port 20, 53, **98, 103**
Lowestoft 37, 65, 144
Lyme Regis 96, 149
Lymington 49, 63, 117, 148
Lympne 71, 146
Lynmouth 92, 93, 150
Lytham St Annes 89, 151

Mablethorpe 19, 144
Maltings 64, 145
Manby, George 126
Maplin Sands 122, 145
Margate 88, 89, 93, 146
Marina 58, 85, **87**, 96; Brighton 85, 94, 135, 147; Haslar **86**; Hythe 85, 130, **132**, 147, pl.11; Ocean Village 35, 147; Port Solent 85, **87**, 147
Martello tower 77-8, 117, 145, 146, 154
Maryport 71, 102, 152
Mast pond 109
Meek, Thomas 122
Middlesbrough 99
Mine and mining 16, 18, 27, 44, 56, 57, 100, 113, 149, 151
Milford on Sea 80
Milford Haven 43, 48, 151
Moor Sand 60, 149
Monarchs: Alfred 72; Charles I 49; Charles II 77, 83; Edward I 74; Elizabeth I 38, 76, 116, 119; George III 87, 148, 88; George V 83; Harold I 22, 73; Henry VII 115; VIII 74, 75, 79, 95, 102, 119, 121; Victoria 87, 88, 130; William I 11, 22, 73, 115; William III 116, 117
Montrose 27,42, 43, 96, 130, 154
Morecombe Bay 91, 152
Mote of Mark 61, 152
Mould loft 108
Mousehole 135, 149
Mucking 21
Museum & Heritage Sites
   Bucklers Hard Museum 108, 149, pl.13
   Chatham Historic Dockyard 108, 145
   Dover Museum 146
   Eastney Beam Engine House 54, 147
   Flag Fen 17, 144
   Grace Darling Museum 142
   Greenock, HM Customs & Excise 117, 152
   Hartlepool Historic Docks 143
   Hull Town Docks Museum 43, 144
   Lancaster Museum 116, 151
   Marine Life Centre and Fishing Museum 38
   Merseyside Maritime Museum 41, 83, 151; HM Customs & Excise 117, 151